LEICESTER
in the 1960s
Ten Years that Changed a City

STEPHEN BUTT

AMBERLEY

First published 2015

Amberley Publishing
The Hill, Stroud
Gloucestershire, GL5 4EP

www.amberley-books.com

British Library Cataloguing in Publication Data.
A catalogue record for this book is available from the British Library.

ISBN 978 1 4456 4057 0 (print)
ISBN 978 1 4456 4090 7 (ebook)

Typesetting and Origination by Amberley Publishing.
Printed in Great Britain.

Introduction

We all have our own history, a personal perception of the past that has been influenced and coloured by many different experiences. Social historians often generalise, using statistics to support their observations. It is written that Leicester in the 1960s was a prosperous city and a place of opportunity. It must have been so because the statistics inform us that there were less than 3,000 people unemployed across the entire city, the big textile and hosiery manufacturers were running at full capacity and the demand for labour meant decent wages, and money in the pocket to buy all you needed from a flourishing high street.

For some of Leicester's citizens this was certainly the case, but not for all. The Employment Exchange in Charles Street, the largest such building in the country by floor area, was still very active. There were still many streets of slums to be cleared in the Victorian residential areas of the city and, further out on the new sprawling council house estates, there were those who for various reasons were not part of the prosperity of the decade.

As with the decade that preceded it, the 1960s was a period of great social and economic change. Life changed for everyone. Over 2,000 railway stations closed as the motor vehicle grew in popularity and availability, National Service ended and colour television became available.

The decade has been described in many ways and it was certainly a revolution in social attitudes, reflected in the popular music of the time, in fashion and in the print and broadcast media.

Revolution always brings conflict in its wake. The Swinging Sixties saw a social conflict within families between parents and children, and within schools between teachers and pupils. Other institutions, notably the Church, found much to be concerned about with the new ideas and free thinking of the sixties generation, and almost every adult over the age of thirty disapproved of the outrageous behaviour and dubious values of the new pop stars, as well as being frightened by the deity-like attention given to them by the young. It was in March 1966 that John Lennon made his remark that The Beatles had become more popular than Jesus Christ. Despite the controversy that the remark provoked, more so in the USA than in Britain, many people in the Established Church silently agreed.

The BBC was another national institution that struggled to keep up with the speed of social change. The corporation's response to pop music was mainly the BBC Northern Dance Orchestra and the Cliff Adams Singers performing cover versions of the bestselling songs of the day and the previous fifty years, whereas the vast majority of teenagers were listening to the real thing on Radio Luxembourg and from the extensive flotilla of pirate radio stations located off the shores of the UK. It was not until 1967 that the BBC finally accepted that its future audience were those millions

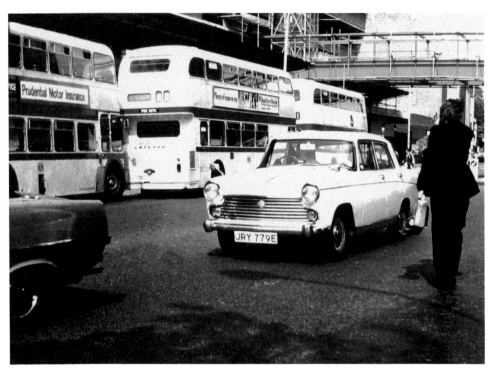

A busy Humberstone Gate, looking towards Charles Street, with the bridge between Lewis's and the Haymarket Centre under construction.

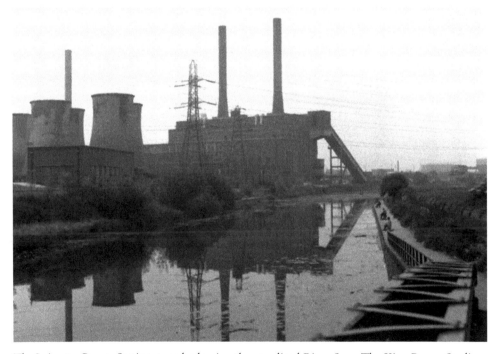

The Leicester Power Station overshadowing the canalised River Soar. The King Power Stadium stands here now. The cooling towers were a familiar sight to football fans at nearby Filbert Street.

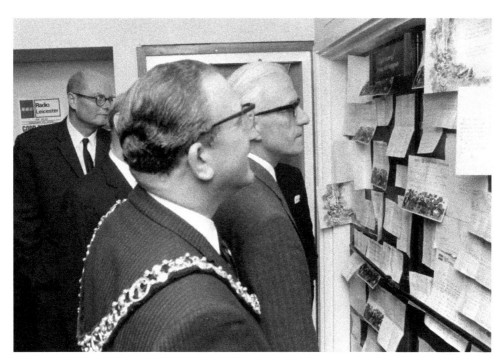

The Lord Mayor of Leicester, Sir Mark Henig, the Postmaster-General, the Rt Hon Edward Short (*right*), and Sir Hugh Greene, BBC Director-General of the BBC (*left*), at the opening of BBC Radio Leicester on 8 November 1967.

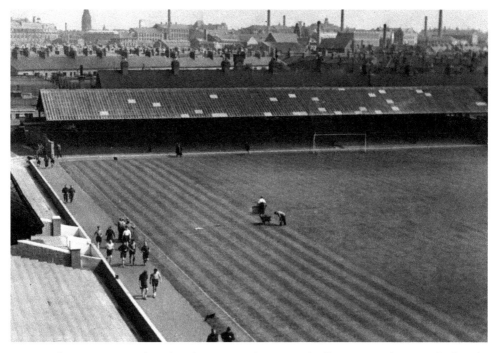

Factory chimneys outnumber church spires in this view of Filbert Street photographed in the 1960s, with the still-industrial skyline of Leicester in the background.

who were not listening to the BBC Light Programme. As a result of the government's Marine Offences Bill, which sank most of the pirate radio stations, the disc jockeys came ashore and formed an almost-orderly queue outside Broadcasting House.

In 1967, the BBC published posters and leaflets to publicise the launch of their first local radio station, which was to be located in Leicester. The corporation ran a prize draw to win one of twenty 'deluxe' VHF radio sets, inviting Leicester people to identify five local 'celebrities'. The personalities that were chosen, presumably as representative of the culture of the city, were comedian Bill Maynard, actor Norman Bird, Tony Lock – captain of Leicestershire County Cricket Club, John Sjoberg – captain of Leicester City, and Englebert Humperdinck. Norman Bird had actually never lived or worked in Leicester. He was born in Coalville and lived for most of his life in the West Midlands. Possibly one of his most memorable and significant roles was as a taxi driver in Richard Attenborough's *Shadowlands*. Bill Maynard was born in Surrey, was educated in Kibworth and has been living in Burbage for some years.

It was a complex and confusing decade for those whose teenage years were the 1960s. Everything that they were being taught, in school and at home, were the values of the previous generation, but all around them was a new culture – exciting, colourful and inspirational.

On the political landscape, responsibility for British policy during the 1960s was shared between the Conservative Government of 1951–64 and the Labour Government of 1964–70. Anticipating a new period of change internationally, Harold Macmillan gave his 'Winds of Change' speech in South Africa in February 1960, forecasting a rise in national consciousness. There were three prime ministers during the period – Macmillan (1957–63), Home (1963/64) and Wilson (1964–70). General elections were held in 1959, 1964, 1966 and 1970. During the 1959–64 Parliament, the Conservatives held a majority of just short of 100. At the start of the 1964–66 Parliament, the Labour Government had an overall majority of just three and, during the 1966–70 Parliaments, a majority of around 100.

The Labour administration from 1964 saw several fundamental social reforms, which included the abolition of capital punishment and the liberalisation of laws on abortion, censorship, divorce, homosexuality and immigration.

As well as the long cold winter of 1962/3, which tested its resources and infrastructure, the country became preoccupied in the Profumo Affair, which rocked political circles in 1961; the Great Train Robbery of 8 August 1963; and the Aberfan Disaster on 21 October 1966, when 116 children and 28 adults were killed by the collapse of a colliery spoil tip.

Although there was massive social change in Britain throughout the decade, the governments of the 1960s were preoccupied in fighting a decline in economic health. There were rising public expectations of higher living standards due to the visible signs of prosperity, but the wider picture revealed that the country was becoming less competitive in world markets, and the consumers of the 1960s were buying more and more imported products. Instead of a clear plan to boost the home economy, the Conservative governments up to 1964, and the Labour governments for the remainder of the decade, became absorbed in fighting an increasing balance of payments deficit and growing public disillusionment. The electors expected more and better from the politicians. When this expectation was not realised, even staunch supporters of one particular political party began considering defection.

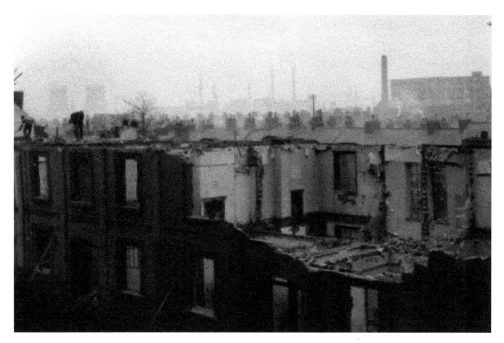

Looking south from the Hawthorn Building of what is now De Montfort University. This photograph records the demolition of terraced housing in the area of Mill Lane and Asylum Street in 1959. The cooling towers of the power station can be seen on the horizon.

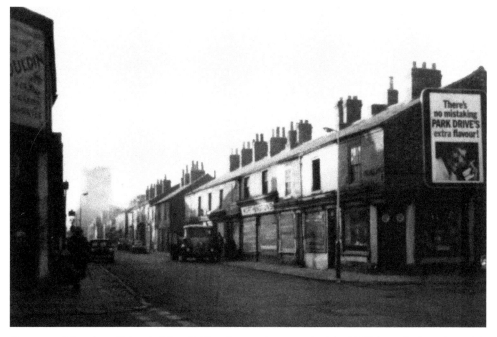

Shops awaiting demolition in New Bridge Street photographed in 1968 from its junction with Joseph Street. The view is towards the power station. Until the late 1950s, Worthingtons Cash Stores traded from Nos 99 and 101. Next door (towards the camera) were Allen's Stores, Frederick O'Donnell, fruiterer, and Eric Hollis, butcher.

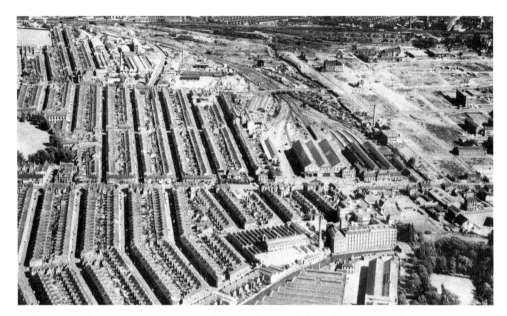

Belgrave Road is running east–west in this aerial view of the Belgrave area of Leicester in 1960. In the foreground are Abbey Park and the Wolsey Knitwear factory. On the right is the Wharf Street slum clearance area awaiting redevelopment to become the St Matthew's Estate.

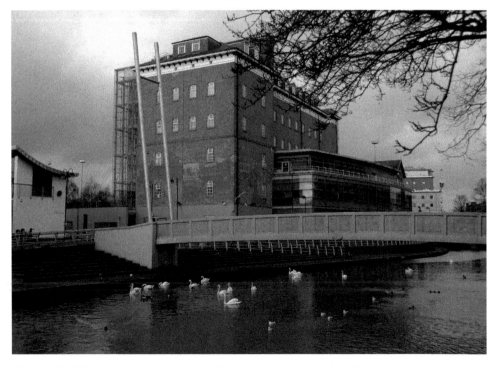

The Pex Building overlooking the Riverside was built in the 1840s. The famous sock company was a major Leicester manufacturer in the 1960s, but all three of the city's factories were closed in 1999 when manufacturing was moved to Romania.

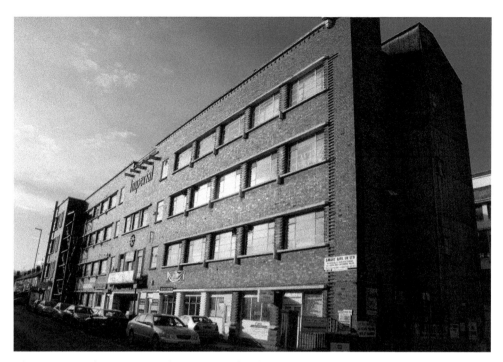

The impressive former Imperial Typewriters headquarters on East Park Road. This is a building which still makes a bold statement. It was designed by the Leicester firm of Pick, Everard, Keay & Gimson.

It was also a decade of great scientific and technological achievement. In 1960, the British Aircraft Corporation was formed out of the old Vickers-Armstrong, Bristol and English Electric companies. Nine years later, Concorde, the world's first and only supersonic passenger airliner, took off on its maiden flight. In 1961, Yuri Gagarin became the first man in space. The Skylark rocket launch from Woomera in South Australia placed the first Leicester-built instrument into space and marked the start of a long-running and successful research programme studying the link between X-radiation from the Sun and radio propagation in the Earth's atmosphere. Before the decade ended, men were walking on the moon. Such achievements changed the way we thought about this planet and ourselves. Our horizons were forced to expand. It was not only this world that could be our oyster.

1

At School and at Work

For most young children, the first time that they had experienced a day away from home and their mother was their first day at primary school, although there was some pre-school or nursery provision available in the 1960s. For those who lived in the Victorian and Edwardian suburbs, this normally involved a walk to a gaunt, red-brick school building. For the children of families who had moved to one of the post-war estates, a 'modern' school of concrete and glass awaited them.

At least the young people who left school in the 1960s and were about to begin their working life in Leicester could be assured of finding employment, as the city's industries and economy were booming.

Schools

The eleven-plus has always provoked controversy. It became an emblem of class distinction and social exclusion, yet it was also seen as a valuable tool for providing social mobility because it based school selection on intellectual ability rather than on the ability of parents to pay. Harold Wilson, Edward Heath, James Callaghan, Margaret Thatcher and John Major were all products of the grammar school, not the public school, system. The eleven-plus examination included written papers in English and arithmetic, and verbal and non-verbal reasoning papers designed to test a child's ability to solve problems and puzzles.

In most schools, the formality of the previous decades remained. All children wore a school uniform in the school colours. Children sat at desks in rows, and at the front of the room stood the teacher, his or her only aids being a blackboard and chalk. With the formality came discipline. Primary schools had few other facilities, no gymnasium or sports hall, no library and often no dining area. Children would walk from their school to a nearby church hall for school dinners, delivered by vans from a central catering unit.

Until the 1960s, the formality continued beyond the eleven-plus. In many grammar schools the masters wore gowns. School uniforms were strictly enforced and subjects taught emphasised the classics including Latin and sometimes Greek. The morning assembly at the start of each day was a Christian service, but those pupils from families of the Roman Catholic or Jewish faiths did not attend. The house system was still in use, with inter-house competitions.

The cultural conflict that was beginning to form could be seen in the principles being taught in many schools. In history, there were still classes in the 1960s where Creationism was still being taught and Darwin was seldom mentioned. Children were still being told that the principal difference between animals and humans was that humans had a soul, and that the world had been created in 4004 BC. Most grammar schools were single-sex, and in the boys' schools pupils were always addressed by only their surnames.

The 1960s saw a fundamental shift in the structure of state education in the UK from grammar and secondary modern schools to what was termed comprehensive education. In 1956 Leicestershire had launched its 'Leicestershire experiment', in which all the children in an area moved at the age of eleven to a high school for three years. The brightest then transferred at the age of fourteen to a grammar school, while the remaining pupils stayed for one further year in their high school and then left for the world of employment. The plan was influential in moving forward the national debate, but any major change was still a long way off. In 1965, the traditional system was further reinforced with the introduction of the Certificate of Secondary Education (CSE) for children who were regarded as incapable of gaining academic success by sitting the General Certificate of Education (GCE).

The city of Leicester did not share the county's enthusiasm for a comprehensive style of education in its schools, and as a result the government prevented the city from spending any money on secondary school building. Leicester was proud of its traditional grammar schools, such as Wyggeston Boys' School and Alderman Newton's School. It was only in 1969 that Leicester finally followed the national trend and put forward plans for reorganisation to Whitehall, which included changing the age at which pupils transferred from primary school to twelve, creating co-educational schools for twelve to sixteen-year-olds, and setting up three sixth-form colleges for those who wished to stay on and prepare for university or college.

It was the frequently changing national political leadership that caused a very uneven and patchy transition to the comprehensive system, which was completed only in the first years of the 1970s. For many Leicester children of the 1960s, their school was a culture set apart from the realities of life.

Industry and Employment

No era or decade is truly 'golden' for all, but the early years of the 1960s were certainly the most prosperous in the city's history for the broadest cross-section of the population. At the beginning of the 1960s, industry and manufacturing in Leicester was expanding, generating a demand for both skilled and unskilled workers and offering comparatively high wages. Feeding that demand were migrants from other cities in the UK, and as a result Leicester's immigrant population began to rise substantially.

Led by the famous names in Leicester's textile, knitwear and hosiery manufacturing businesses including Nathaniel Corah & Sons, T. W. Kempton, Faire Brothers, Wolsey Knitwear, Pick's, Cherub, Byford's, Pex and De Montfort Knitwear, as well as the famous shoe manufacturers and retailers and the mighty British United Shoe Machinery Co. (BUSMC) – with its extensive headquarters and factories bordering the Belgrave Road – Leicester in the 1960s was a place of prosperity. For most of the twentieth century the BUSMC was the world's largest manufacturer of footwear machinery and materials, and exported shoe machinery and technology to more than fifty countries. During the 1960s it was the largest employer in Leicester with more than 4,500 people working for the company.

In 1961, with a population of 273,470, the unemployment rate was little more than 1 per cent. It was a figure that had not changed significantly since the mid-fifties when the lowest ever post-war national unemployment figure of just 215,000 had been recorded.

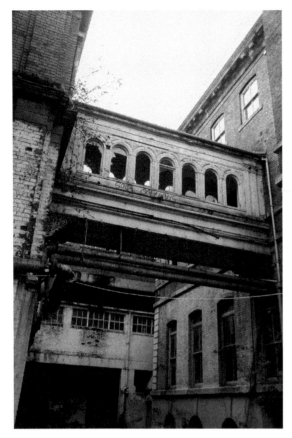

Left: Part of Corah's St Margaret's factory complex, photographed in 2015 – neglected and in a dangerous condition.

Below: Christmas celebrations during the 1960s in the 'J' Department of Corah's St Margaret's works.

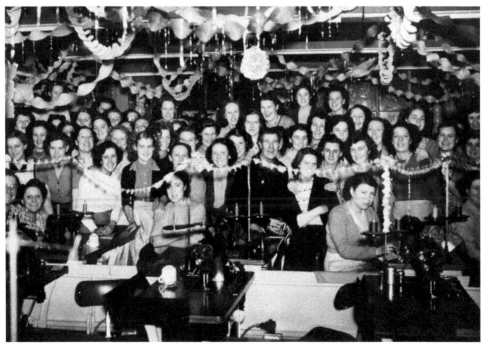

In the High Streets of most cities and towns in the UK, Leicester-based retailers were dominant, indicating the strength of Leicester's economy. Shoe retailers included Stead & Simpson and Freeman, Hardy & Willis, and Marks & Spencer was a major retailer of knitwear manufactured by the Corah group. Kendall & Sons were selling their umbrellas, rainwear and ladies' clothing through their 100 shops, and other companies with roots in the Leicester area included Curry's and Wilkinson.

In 1961, Corah opened two new factories in Leicester, at Sanvey Gate, producing men's socks, and the Corella Works in nearby Junior Street manufactured seamless stockings. In 1963, the company took over Fosse Knitwear Ltd and its factory in Parker Drive. In 1965, the company was planning an estimated output that year for Marks & Spencer in excess of 3,996,000 dozens of garments, socks and tights across their factories. Fosse Knitwear accounted for over 47,000 items of women's knitwear and tights.

Leicester's industries, many based in Victorian buildings and some with production facilities that dated to the time of the industrial revolution, were hungry for energy and wasteful in how they used it. Coal was still the peak supplier of power, and would remain so until the discovery of gas beneath the North Sea. Although modern electrically powered machines had largely replaced the old steam-powered devices, coal was still needed to generate electricity. Most households in Leicester still used coal to heat their homes, even those with central heating, and coal, in the form of steam power, was still the principal means of moving goods across the country.

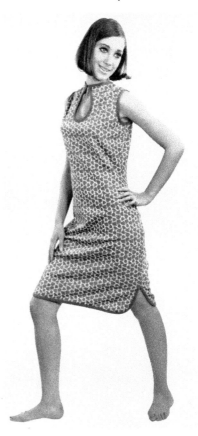

A Corah marketing image from 1965, promoting the 'St Margaret's Gem' girl buying outfits made of artificial fibres to supplement the wool and cotton in her wardrobe.

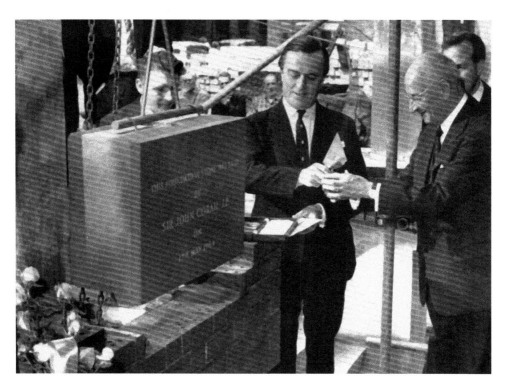

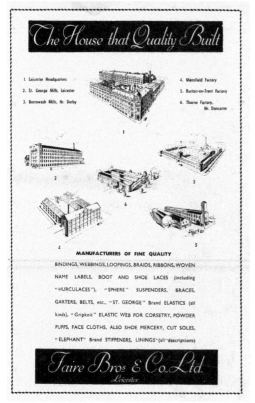

Above: An extension to Corah's St Margaret's works being laid on 27 May 1965 by Sir John Corah, with W. G. Turriff, chairman of the Warwick-based Turriff Construction Group.

Left: Founded in 1855, Faire Bros was a major employer in Leicester and elsewhere when they were taken over in 1967. Their Leicester factory and offices were extensive.

Out in the Leicestershire coalfield, the mines were still focused on expansion. Between 1961 and 1963 a sloping drift was constructed at Snibston Colliery in Coalville, measuring 925 yards in length. It connected the underground workings with the surface and replaced the old Stephenson Shaft in which miners and coal had to be wound up and down. The investment continued with a new coal preparation plant on the surface and an expansion in the railways sidings. Additional tunnels were bored to connect neighbouring mines including Whitwick with Snibston. The National Coal Board was clearly looking forward to an economically viable future, as in 1967 the pithead baths were refurbished and new offices, workshops and medical centre were constructed. Throughout the decade, the mine's output broke all records and reached its peak during the week ending 18 January 1969 when it produced 16,104 tonnes.

However, by the end of the decade, the rosy picture of near full employment, and a manufacturing base that dominated markets across the country and further afield, was fading. In 1960, Britain's manufacturers held almost 20 per cent of world markets and dominated the home market. This country had iconic world-class products such as the Triumph motorcycle, the Mini and the Comet airliner. Ten years later, Britain was in a state of decline, which brought with it discontent and industrial action, and governments who could find no effective solution to the dramatic decline in Britain's industrial and manufacturing output.

The causes of the decline were many and complex, and reached back a full decade to the state of the world economy immediately after the Second World War. Countries that had suffered major damage to their manufacturing infrastructure during the war,

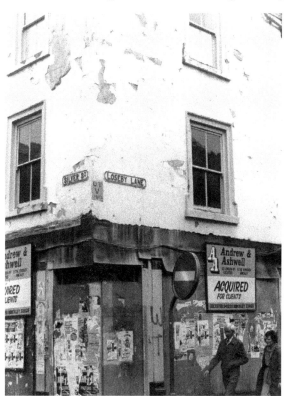

In the 1960s, when this photograph was taken, this building at the junction of Loseby Lane and Silver Street, opposite the Globe Public House, was in poor repair.

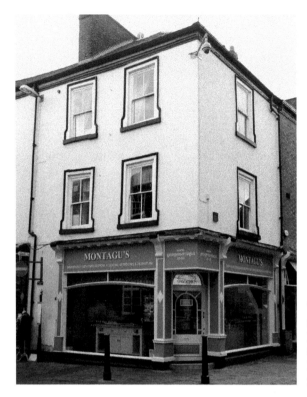

Throughout the decade, the old town, now known as the 'Leicester Lanes', remained largely ignored by the planners, but pedestrianisation has brought refurbishment and has revitalised this area considerably.

when factories and sources of power had been deliberately targeted by enemy bombers, had now rebuilt, and with modern manufacturing processes they were beginning to compete with Britain's world trade dominance. The countries of the Commonwealth on whom Britain had always relied as trading partners were looking to wider markets, and at home the development of the National Health Service and the wider concept of the 'welfare state' meant the need for increased taxation.

The effect on Leicester was that the cost of the public services and new infrastructure expected by the public overwhelmed the city's finances. By the autumn of 1963, the city was £43 million in debt because of the necessary expenditure on education, public health and housing.

By the end of the 1960s, the exuberant expansion of Leicester's industries had ceased. In its place came increasing industrial strife and a society in which management, trade unions and politicians grew apart and treated each other with deep antagonism.

Leicester Polytechnic

For many young people of school leaving age, family custom influenced whether they moved on to further education or went out to work. Many girls followed their mothers and grandmothers into the textile and hosiery industry. For young men, the manufacturing industry provided clerical jobs. Others could learn practical skills at local colleges, and some, who had been taught in the grammar schools, aspired to go to university.

In 1966, the new high-rise Fletcher building in the Newarke was opened by Her Majesty The Queen Mother, and in that same year the white paper *A Plan for*

Polytechnics and Other Colleges was published. On 1 April 1969, the Leicester Regional College of Art and Technology, which, as two separate colleges, had a history that reached back to the 1880s, became the City of Leicester Polytechnic. It was located on two sites, the Newarke, in the heart of Leicester, and Scraptoft, a former teacher-training college on the outskirts.

The government intended that these institutions would ensure working-class communities benefited from the expansion of higher education. They served their local communities rather than attracting students from further afield and offered more vocational-oriented qualifications that had a relevance to the industrial base of the area.

The polytechnic continued to run courses that would feed into the business and commercial needs of the city, but those needs were changing dramatically and the polytechnic needed to follow suit. In addition, the institution added music and drama courses. The teaching staff including the influential composer Gavin Briars, whose legacy to some extent has fed through to the respected musical technology courses offered by De Montfort University today. The highly successful Leicester Comedy Festival also began within the polytechnic, created by Scraptoft student Geoff Rowe, who still directs the festival. The polytechnic had the right to bestow degree awards between 1969 and 1992, when it became De Montfort University.

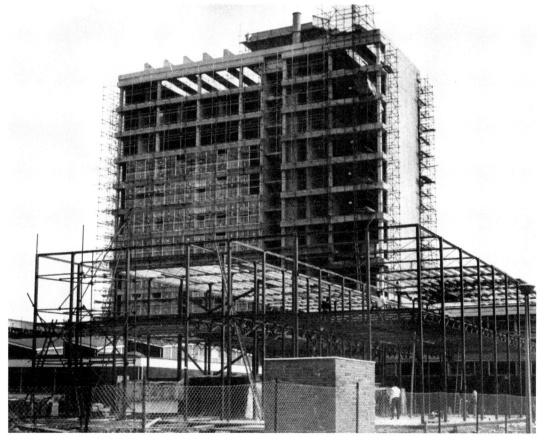

A view of the construction of the Fletcher Building in the Newarke in the early years of the 1960s.

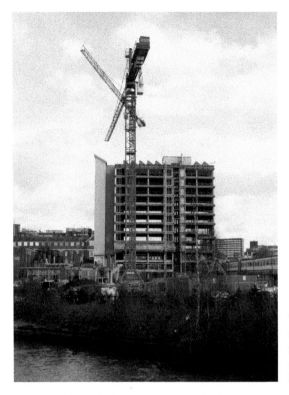

The high-rise Fletcher Building on the campus of De Montfort University in the Newarke. It was completed in 1966 and is undergoing major redevelopment in 2015.

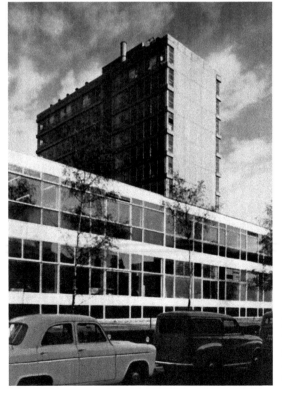

Brave new architecture of the academic world. A view of the Fletcher Building in the Newarke immediately prior to the opening of the complex by HRH The Queen Mother in 1966.

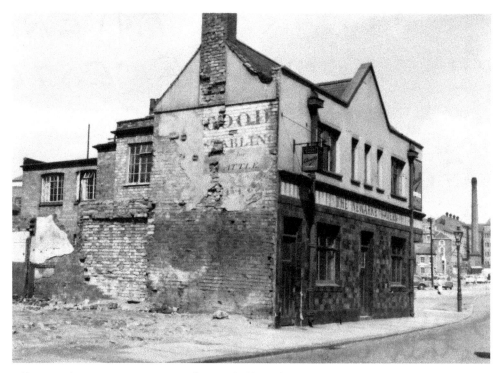

The Newarke Tavern at No. 73 Mill Lane, halfway between Grey Street and Cardigan Street. The Fletcher buildings now occupy much of this area of the Newarke.

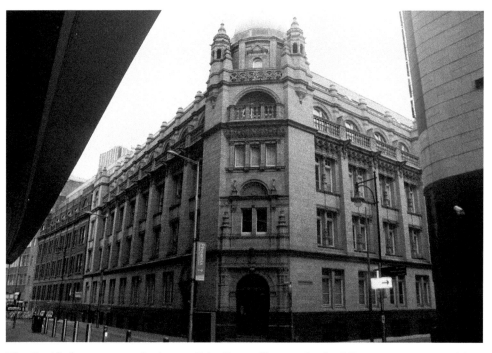

The dignified entrance to the former Faire Bros offices on Rutland Street, now converted into apartments in the heart of the city's Cultural Quarter, and overlooked by the Curve theatre.

University of Leicester

The former University College of Leicester was granted its Royal Charter in 1957 to become a fully fledged university with the right to award its own degrees. There followed a period of expansion in student numbers and degree courses offered which required the construction of a number of new purpose-built buildings on the campus south of the city. The Percy Gee student union building was opened by Her Royal Highness The Queen on 9 May 1958, but in the 1960s the skyline of the university campus was changed with the erection of three remarkable and distinctive towers – the Department of Engineering, designed by architects Stirling & Gowan; the Attenborough tower, designed by Sir Philip Dowson of Arup Associates with Ove Arup as consulting engineers and constructed by John Laing Construction Ltd in 1968-1970; and the Charles Wilson building, designed by Sir Denys Lasdun in 1963.

The university's engineering building was the first major building by British architect James Stirling, and comprises workshops and laboratories at ground level and a tower containing offices and lecture theatres. It was completed in 1963 and is notable for the way in which its external form reflects its internal functions. The Attenborough tower houses the tallest working paternoster in the UK.

Two distinguished writers used their experiences of life at Leicester University in the years immediate before the 1960s for their novels. It is claimed that Kingsley Amis was inspired to write *Lucky Jim* (published 1954) while visiting his friend Philip Larkin,

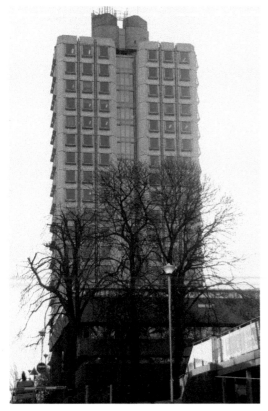

The Attenborough Building of the University of Leicester. At eighteen storeys, it is the tallest building on the campus, designed by Ove Arup and constructed 1968–70. In Pesvner's opinion 'prickly with window units angled out from top to bottom of the pre-cast concrete panels, a feature more successful inside than out.'

who was working in the university library. Malcolm Bradbury, who had read English at Leicester in the 1950s, also based his satire *Eating People is Wrong* (published 1959) on the university.

Vaughan College

The association between Vaughan College, founded by Revd David Vaughan in 1862 and University College Leicester, dates back to the 1920s, and it was a partnership that grew closer in the decades which followed. The central ring road system, which had begun in the mid-1950s, required the demolition of the former Vaughan College building, and it was one of the university's pro-vice-chancellors, Alderman Charles Keene, who suggested a purpose-built building combining a museum alongside the Jewry Wall archaeological site. It was completed in 1962 to a design by Trevor Dannatt.

The innovative building provided Vaughan College with a modern, purpose-built building for an expanding staff that provided full-time, day release and part-time courses. Under the dynamic leadership of Dennis Rice, who was appointed as warden in 1962, the college thrived. One of Rice's many innovations during the 1960s was the use of the common area for art exhibitions. Local artists could exhibit for free, in return for donating a picture selected by the warden. Over the years, a fine collection of local art developed.

The St Nicholas Circle buildings served the college well until 2013 when the University of Leicester announced its intention to transfer the Vaughan College operation to the main campus. In 2014, the buildings were empty and for sale.

2

Sport

Gary Lineker was born in Leicester in 1960. David Gower was three years old when the decade began and Martin Johnson was not even a faint spark in his parents' eyes. The 'golden age' of Leicester's sports had been born and it would take time for their skills to mature and be recognised.

In the 1960s, the popularity of football seemed unassailable. Although Leicester City was relegated towards the end of the decade, it was an era that saw many exciting matches and a quality game at Filbert Street. It was a similar story at Welford Road and Grace Road, with teams that saw a reincarnation and a revival in fortunes as the decade progressed. For Leicester's other sports, it was a different story.

Football

For many sport historians, the 1960s were the golden years nationally and internationally, with players of exceptional ability and charisma including George Best, Bobby Moore, Jack Charlton and Pelé. The absolute peak of the decade for English fans came on 30 July 1966 at 5.00 p.m. when, thanks to a final goal from Geoff Hurst, England won the World Cup in London at the Wembley Stadium.

Similar shining performances were witnessed at Filbert Street. Their home since it was laid out in 1891, Leicester City Football Club bought the freehold of the ground in 1962 for £30,500. The club had invested in floodlights five years earlier.

For almost all the decade, the club was under the management of Matt Gillies, who had been appointed on 8 November 1958 and remained in post until resigning on 30 November 1968 to be succeeded by Frank O'Farrell. The Foxes reached the FA Cup final in 1961 and 1963 but lost both matches. Having lost in 1961 to double winners Tottenham, the club were England's representatives in the 1961/62 European Cup Winners' Cup.

It was in the 1962/63 season that they reached the top of the First Division after a remarkable performance in a series of games played on frozen pitches, which earned the Foxes the nickname of the 'Ice Kings'. The winter months of that season were the coldest on record since the beginning of the twentieth century, with temperatures as low as -16C recorded in some areas. No First Division match was played in England during January 1963 and Leicester did not play a game between Boxing Day (1962) and 9 February 1963. Many games across the country were cancelled, while the most prosperous clubs resorted to some ingenious means of thawing out their pitches, including the use of motorway tar-burning vehicles.

At Filbert Street, groundsman Bill Taylor pre-empted the chill by feeding the top soil with a mixture of fertiliser and weed killer, creating a chemical reaction that created

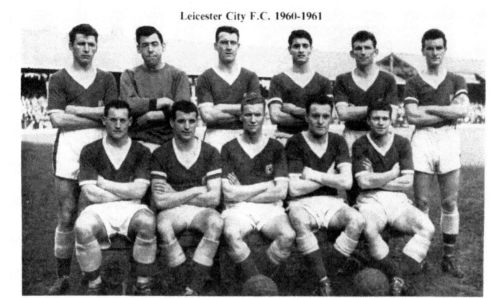

Leicester City F.C. 1960-1961

Back row (*left to right*): LEN CHALMERS, GORDON BANKS, IAN KING, FRANK McLINTOCK, COLIN APPLETON, RICHARD NORMAN.
Front row (*left to right*): HOWARD RILEY, KEN LEEK, JIMMY WALSH, KEN KEYWORTH, ALBERT CHEESEBROUGH
(*Photo courtesy Sports Mercury, Leicester*)

Above: The Leicester City team for the 1960/61 season, with legendary names including Gordon Banks and Frank McLintock on the back row. The others are immediately recognisable by City fans.

Right: A great day and a memorable date in the Foxes history: Saturday 6 May 1961 at Wembley Stadium, the FA Challenge Cup against Spurs. The Foxes lost 2-0.

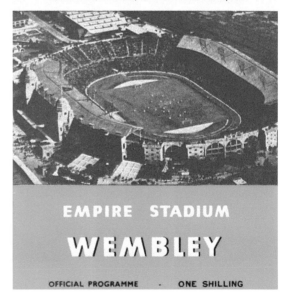

THE FOOTBALL ASSOCIATION CHALLENGE CUP COMPETITION

FINAL TIE
LEICESTER CITY
v
TOTTENHAM HOTSPUR

SATURDAY, MAY 6th, 1961   KICK-OFF 3 p.m.

EMPIRE STADIUM
WEMBLEY

OFFICIAL PROGRAMME   ·   ONE SHILLING

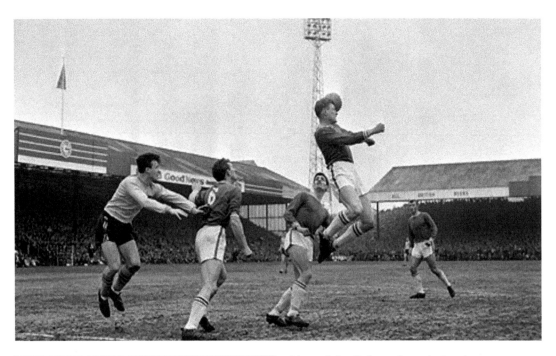

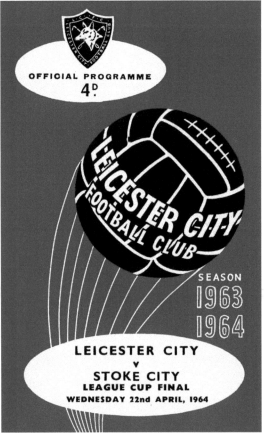

Above: John Sjoberg clears during the 1962/63 FA quarter final against Norwich City on 30 March 1963. The Foxes won 2-0 and went on to beat Liverpool 1-0, but lost to Manchester United 3-1 in the final. Sjoberg retired to manage a printing firm based initially in the former Great Central Railway station buildings.

Left: Another memorable event for Foxes fans, the 1964 League Cup final against Stoke City. This is the programme for the second leg. Leicester won this match 3-2, winning the Cup 4-3 on aggregate.

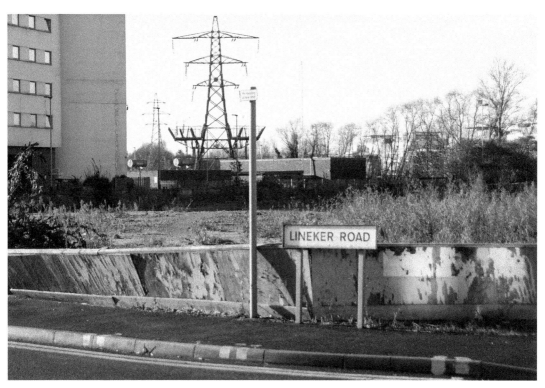

The site of the Filbert Street ground in 2015. Development of Lineker Road including student accommodation was cancelled because of the financial recession.

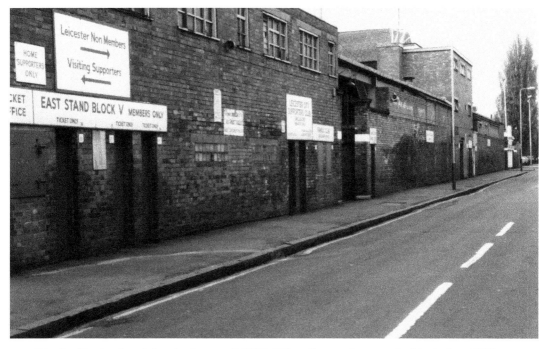

The familiar landmark for city fans until 2002: Filbert Street, photographed in the late 1960s.

enough heat to prevent the ice from taking hold. The snow was cleared by an army of fans recruited through the *Leicester Mercury*, straw was then spread over the grass, and Taylor sat up all night before matches keeping twelve coke-powered braziers burning. Despite such lateral thinking and experience, even these measures were insufficient in the first weeks of that year.

After the thaw they enjoyed a lengthy unbeaten run, reaching the top of the Division with nine games still to be played. Unfortunately, performances then slipped and the Foxes ended the season in a disappointing fourth place, but their highest finish since the war.

In 1964, they won the League Cup for the first time, beating Stoke 4-3 on aggregate and reached the final twelve months later, losing to Chelsea 3-2 on aggregate. Despite such glories, Matt Gillies resigned in November 1968 after a poor start to the season. The Foxes were relegated but went on to reach the FA Cup final in 1969 under Frank O'Farrell, losing to Manchester City 1-0.

Rugby

Apart from the annual Boxing Day encounter with the Barbarians, gates at the Welford Road ground in the 1960s were usually between 1,000 and 2,000, compared with a possible capacity of nearly 18,000. Numbers remained fairly steady throughout the decade, although by the end of 1969 the club had less than 700 members.

In November 1967, the Tigers gained a wider local audience with the opening of BBC Radio Leicester, which provided match commentaries and interviews live from the ground presented by the legendary Van Hopkins. Van was headmaster at the Lancaster Boys' School, but also closely associated with the club. He joined the Tigers' committee in the mid-1960s and later become their social secretary. He was the mainstay of the radio station's rugby coverage from its inception until 1987, when he was succeeded

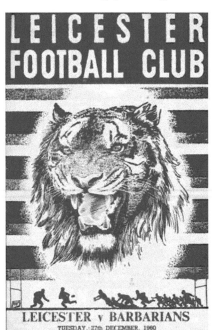

The traditional Boxing Day encounter between Leicester Tigers and the Barbarians began in 1909. It continued until 2006, with one further game in 2014 in Tigers' 125th season.

by Bleddyn Jones. Bleddyn played for the Tigers from 1969, making 333 appearances for the club.

It was in 1968 that one of the most influential characters ever to bring his skills to Welford Road was appointed coach. Herbert Victor 'Chalkie' White also taught at Nottingham High School, but his forward thinking approach, in a still amateur game where coaching was viewed in some quarters as cheating, influenced the Tigers for many years. He encouraged the players to consider strategy and to think about tactics, as well as instigating a stronger fitness and training regime. His personal approach to the game and unique style of coaching, along with the standards he set, introduced the word 'professionalism' to Welford Road. As the Tigers' games improved, so too did the Saturday afternoon attendances.

Cricket

In 1960, the Grace Road ground was still the playing field of the City of Leicester Boys' School. Cricket matches were therefore limited to just four games during the school term. This forced the club to play at grounds elsewhere in the county including Hinckley and Ashby-de-la-Zouch in order to fulfil their list of first-class fixtures. It was not until 1965 that Leicestershire County Cricket Club was able to purchase the ground from the Leicester City Council at a cost of £24,000.

The purchase enabled investment in the ground to begin. The Meet was made into two floors with a 130-foot Long Room upstairs that included a dance floor. A new pavilion was completed before the start of the 1966 season and signalled years of redevelopment. 1969 saw a conversion that enabled the Long Room to be used as nets during the winter. A members' bar was constructed from the rooms formerly used as changing rooms for the Second XI, and trees were planted around

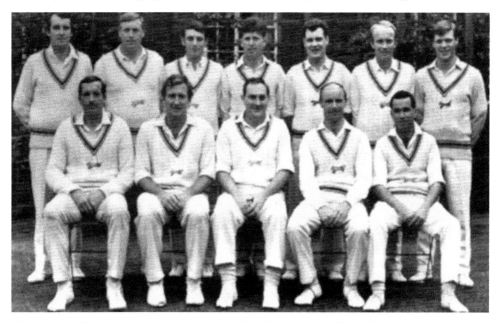

The Leicestershire County Cricket in 1969 under the captaincy of Ray Illingworth, who moved from Yorkshire in that year.

the perimeter of the ground – the gift of Dennis Butler, the 9th Earl of Lanesborough, who had owned the 3000-acre Swithland Estate. In 1969, new entrance gates at the Park Hill Drive entrance were given by E. E. Snow and at the Curzon Road entrance by S. T. Hickling.

Edward Eric Snow, a brother of the scientist and novelist C. P. Snow, wrote the first major history of Leicestershire County Cricket, which was published in Leicester in 1949. He went on to compile many of the club's yearbooks, including those of 1964–66 in association with Mike Turner. As well as being a well-known local businessman, Sydney Hickling played for Leicestershire from 1949 to 1950. An all-round sportsman, he served the club for many years. He died in October 1973, at which time he was the honorary treasurer and vice president.

Speedway

The 1960s were lean years for Speedway enthusiasts and for the Blackbird Road stadium in Leicester. Across the country, many tracks had closed during the previous decade, and Blackbird Road was to follow suit. Under Mike Parker, the Leicester Hunters entered a team in the provincial league in 1962 but ended the season close to the bottom. Takings at the gate were low and the team was transferred to Long Eaton for the following season. It was the Hunters' final season. Although attempts were made in 1963 to reinvigorate the sport through the Pride of the Midlands individual competition, open-licence meetings, and bringing top riders to the track, attendance continued to decline and the stadium was closed in 1964.

Blackbird Road reopened in 1968 under the leadership of Reg Fearman and Ron Wilson, and with the transfer of the Long Eaton operation to Leicester with a new name – the Leicester Lions. At the first meeting of the season the reinvigorated team beat King's Lynn by a remarkable eighteen points. Stock car racing continued spasmodically at Blackbird Road with events in 1962 and 1963. The Lions were to

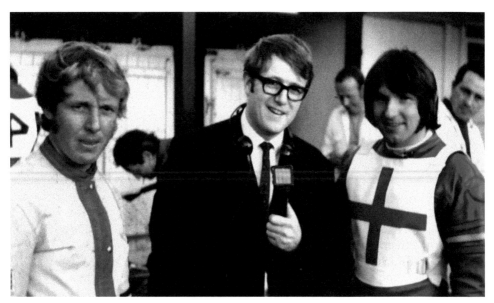

BBC commentator Mike Smith with Speedway riders at the Blackbird Road stadium in 1969.

continue to race at Blackbird Road until 1983 when the stadium was sold to Barratt Homes. It was later demolished to make way for housing.

Basketball

A new professional sport came to Leicestershire in 1967 with the creation of the Loughborough All-Stars Basketball Team, later to become the Leicester Riders. They hold the distinction of being the oldest professional club in British basketball. The team was founded on 26 April 1967 by students and lecturers at Loughborough University, their first regular venue being the town's Victory Hall where matches were held until 1981. The club moved from Loughborough to Leicester in 1981, backed by Leicester City Council and Leicester City Bus (hence the change in nickname to 'Riders'). Matches were played at Granby Halls until its closure in 2000.

Basketball was invented in 1891 in Massachusetts, USA, by Dr James Naismith, a physical education professor as a routine for conditioning young athletes during the winter months. Its popularity grew quickly across America through the college and YMCA networks, and during the First World War the American Expeditionary Force took the game to wherever it was fighting. The game became truly international in 1932 and was an official sport at the 1936 Olympic Games in Berlin.

Roller Skating

Roller skating was a serious sport and a popular form of recreation for children and teenagers in Leicester in the 1960s before the advent of the skateboard. The venue, Leicester's much-loved Granby Halls, was the ideal location. It was within a bus ride or walking distance of many who lived in the city and surrounding housing estates, and it is still sorely missed. Although the sport is still catered for in several out-of-town leisure centres operated by Leicester City Council, there remains no central location which youngsters can reach on foot.

It was a participatory activity and a social occasion, and it catered equally for both those who wanted to train seriously and the many who simply wished for an inexpensive outing with friends. It was a regular Saturday afternoon leisure activity, with the more dedicated participants also attending on Friday and Sunday evenings or on the club night on Mondays. The present Empress Roller Skating Club is a revival of those days.

Social media websites still feature memories of those days, skating to the latest hits which were played on a loud PA system, and being covered with the dust that kicked up from the surface of the rink. For a few, it was the gateway to a professional career in figure, freestyle and dance skating.

Wrestling

Wrestling was a sport that had grown into a popular and widely followed activity due to the effective and regular promotion by Independent Television during the late 1950s. By 1960 it had become a mainstay of their Saturday afternoon *World of Sport* programme, partly owing to its value as an item that could fill the programme at any time when weather or technical difficulties caused other sport coverage to be cancelled.

The famous names on the national circuit included Shirley Crabtree (later to become 'Big Daddy'), Jackie Pallo, Geoff Portz, Masambulla and Billy Two-Rivers. All were cleverly and fiercely promoted and all came to Leicester, appearing at both the De Montfort Hall (on the second Wednesday and fourth Monday of the month) and the Granby Halls. Women in particular were attracted to the matches, particularly the famous 'tag-team' bouts, frequently between the 'Baddies' (Mick McManus and Steve Logan) and the 'Goodies' (The Royal Brothers otherwise known as Bert Royal and Vic Faulkner).

The local 'golden boy' of wrestling in Leicester was Mick Collins. He was just thirteen years of age when he first stepped into the ring at the Granby Halls in January 1961. Another Leicester-based wrestler was Ron Marino, who became a professional in 1963 under local promoter Jack Taylor, having watched the game as a boy accompanying his father to bouts at the Cossington Street baths. Matches took place at Cossington Street on Fridays in the autumn and winter months. Between October and March the baths were drained of water, and covered over by a solid floor. The building could accommodate 1,500 spectators.

3

Music

Although the music of the 1950s was certainly age-specific, and the Teddy boy culture was divisive, it was not until the 1960s that a profound gulf appeared between the music of the younger generation and that of their parents. The music itself, described as 'beat' or 'pop', was not totally new in its form or structure, because it had its roots in soul, skiffle and rhythm and blues. It was all that went with the music, the fashions and the attitudes, that was seen as reactionary by the older generation.

In Leicester, as in other towns and cities across the UK, there was a true diversity of musical forms available in performance and for participation. The De Montfort Hall, which has served the city of Leicester well over the decades, provided a major and accessible concert venue for the wide diversity of musical styles and activities that have prospered in the city and was able to accommodate the new and the traditional. It was not uncommon in the 1960s for a concert by the local Leicester Symphony Orchestra to be followed on the next evening by a chart-topping beat group and a brass band contest, with perhaps a boxing tournament to end the week.

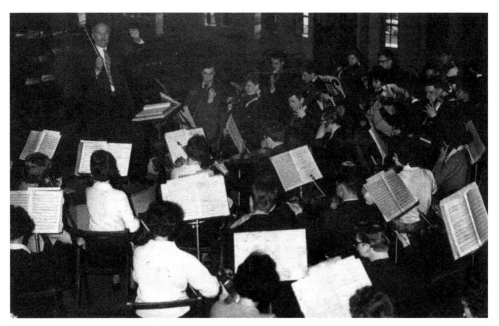

Sir Adrian Boult rehearsing sections of the Leicestershire Schools' Symphony Orchestra, at the De Montfort Hall in 1962.

Leicester's thriving industries and the coal mines of north-west Leicestershire fostered a number of longstanding brass bands. The county council's education service was at the forefront of delivering practical music education in the form of many different ensembles and orchestras to match different levels of children's abilities, and the city's cultural past, with its roots in the benefactors of the Victorian era, was represented by the distinguished Leicester Philharmonic Society.

Popular Music

The new music of the 1960s was as much a social revolution as it was a popular art form. The decade was a milestone in the history of popular music culture in the United Kingdom and much further afield. A merger of musical forms that included skiffle, rock and roll, and American influences such as surf, soul and rhythm and blues, created a very new and, for the teenagers of the time, an incredibly exciting sound that was to develop hand-in-hand with an explosion of new styles in fashion and a revolution in youth culture.

One of the most popular forms of American music, a merger of folk and rock, came to the De Montfort Hall from the state of Tennessee on 17 April 1960. They were the Everly Brothers. They returned to the same venue for six further gigs during the decade. Phil and Don Everly were immensely successful. They were the first of the 'new' pop stars to sign a million-dollar contract, and their output was remarkable, with nine singles in the UK Top Twenty bestselling charts in 1960/61 alone.

The older popular musical forms were still selling in the first years of the decade. Traditional jazz musician Acker Bilk, with the Leon Young String Chorale, enjoyed immense success with his instrumental 'Stranger on the Shore', which reached No. 1 in the USA and No. 2 in the UK charts. Elvis Presley (having just returned to civilian life after two years' service in the US Army), Helen Shapiro, Eden Kane, Ricky Nelson, Billy Fury, Petula Clarke, Frankie Vaughan and the Temperance Seven all released bestselling singles in 1961, and many were to continue to be successful alongside the newcomers.

A notable release in 1962 was 'Telstar' by the Tornados, a rare example of popular music reflecting a topical news story. An instrumental, it was composed by Joe Meek in London and recorded by a group of musicians whom he had hired for the purpose. It was recorded within one hour of the musicians arriving at his studio in North London. Meek had been inspired by the first transatlantic television transmission from the Telstar satellite on 23 July 1962. It caught the mood of the moment, selling over 5 million copies and remaining at the top of the UK charts for three weeks. Tragically, having suffered from depression for some years, Meek committed suicide in 1967.

By 1963, the new bands, chiefly from Merseyside and Manchester were becoming prominent. The Beatles topped the charts, which also included Brian Poole and the Tremeloes, Billy J. Kramer and the Dakotas, Gerry and the Pacemakers, The Bachelors, Freddie and the Dreamers, The Hollies, The Dave Clark Five and The Four Seasons. However, there was still room for Kenny Ball & His Jazzmen and the folk trio Peter, Paul and Mary.

In Woolworths in Leicester in 1960, a 45 rpm single cost 4s 6d. For young teenagers, keeping up with the ever-changing musical scene was an expensive occupation.

Alongside the groups were the solo artists, many of whom were to survive the competition but who needed a change of image and musical style. Leicester's Gerry

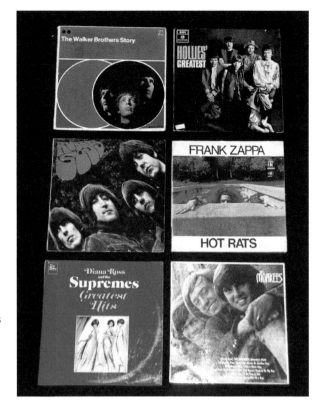

Right: Six iconic vinyl albums from top bands of the 1960s in the UK and USA: The Beatles, The Monkees, the Walker Brothers, The Hollies, The Supremes and Frank Zappa.

Below: This is 'Family', Leicester's forgotten band of the 1960s. Led by Roger Chapman, they performed from early 1967 until late 1973 and were a part of the 1960s psychedelic movement.

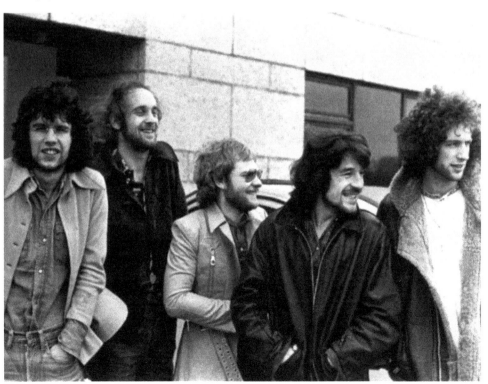

Dorsey became Englebert Humperdinck, and hired a new manager. As a result, in 1967 his single 'Release Me' reached the top of the charts, and prevented The Beatles' groundbreaking 'Strawberry Fields Forever' and 'Penny Lane' from achieving that exalted position. At the peak of its popularity, 'Release Me' sold 85,000 copies every day.

A number of home-grown bands began to make an appearance. Family, led by Roger Chapman, was formed in 1966, creating a form described as progressive rock because of the other genres it explored. The Foresights, another Leicester band, derived their name from the fact that all four members of the group wore spectacles. Leicester's Jon Lord, who was later to find fame with Deep Purple and to pioneer the integration of popular and classical musical forms in composition, joined his first band in 1960 – a London-based jazz ensemble called the Bill Ashton Combo, which included in its line-up, Jack Shephard, later to become an actor and to create the role of ITV's Inspector Wycliffe.

Later in the 1960s, several of the leading British pop musicians embraced 'psychedelia', a growing phenomenon in western culture at a time in which drugs were taken to enhance and change mental awareness. These bands included The Who, Cream, Pink Floyd, and The Beatles.

The United Kingdom won the Eurovision Song Contest twice in the 1960s – in 1967 with Sandie Shaw's 'Puppet on a String', and again in 1969 with 'Boom Bang-a-Bang', sung by Lulu.

Classical Music

Leicester's own orchestra, the Leicester Symphony Orchestra, which had played its first concert at the De Monfort Hall in 1922, entered the 1960s in poor form but with a new musical director. Simeon Iliffe was the orchestra's principal trumpet and had been in the orchestra since 1923. He was also an experienced brass band conductor and performer. Clearly, his fellow players respected him as under Iliffe's baton, the orchestra's quality of performance greatly improved, and by the end of the decade had gained national critical recognition.

Leicester and Leicestershire were firmly on the European classical music map by the 1960s with the success of the Leicestershire Schools Symphony Orchestra. The county's music adviser and founder of the LSSO sought the support of Britain's leading contemporary composer – Sir Michael Tippett – who, in 1965, agreed to be its patron and regular guest conductor.

The orchestra undertook a series of European tours that were remarkable for their extent and the diversity and standard of the music performed, quickly gaining an international reputation. Many other distinguished musicians and composers were to come to Leicester to work with the talented young students, including Sir Adrian Boult, Sir Malcolm Arnold and Norman del Mar. Del Mar was a regular visitor and a fine trainer. His insistence on the highest standards took the orchestra to a new peak in performance in 1968 when he conducted the orchestra in Vienna's Musikverein and the Mozarteum in Salzburg.

The Leicester Philharmonic Society appointed a new conductor in 1961. Trevor Harvey, who had been the director of music to the British Forces Network in Germany, led the choir for most of the decade, and culminated with a performance of Bruckner's 'Mass in F Minor'. During Harvey's years, the 'Phil' also sang under the baton of such distinguished conductors as Sir John Barbirolli, Sir David Wilcocks, Maurice Handford and Sir Adrian Boult.

The Leicester City Male Voice Choir, under the baton of Philip Jenkins, reached a high point in their history in the early 1960s with visits to the International Music Eisteddfod in Llangollen in 1961 and 1962. Despite competing with more experienced choirs, the men from Leicester gained a very satisfactory middle of the table position in the finals. Numbers declined in the latter half of the decade, but the quality of performance improved. The first of what became an annual series of celebrity concerts took place on 10 May 1969, drawing upon local soloists. The choir braved all winds and weathers, including snow, to sing in the Town Hall Square at the annual Lord Mayor of Leicester's Carol Service, a tradition that began in 1960.

David Gwerfyl Davies was appointed music adviser to the Leicester Education Committee in January 1963. In seeking to encourage a greater enthusiasm for teaching music in the city's primary schools, Dr Davies created a choir in order to meet as many of his music teachers as possible in a relatively informal and positive environment. Their first performance was on the stage of the De Montfort Hall in the 1963 carol concert for secondary schools, an annual event which Davies conducted. They were accompanied on the De Montfort Hall organ by the popular and highly respected Leicester organist, Frederick Allt.

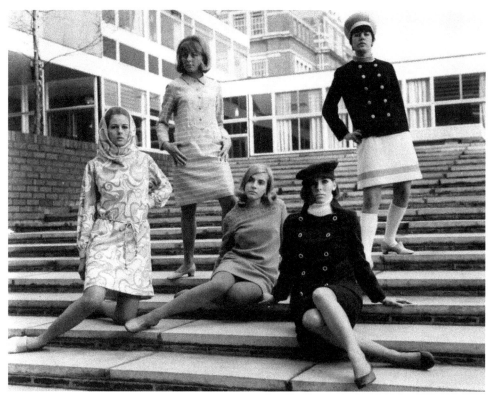

Leicester Polytechnic students modelling their own designs at the opening of the Fletcher Building of Leicester Polytechnic in 1966.

The choir rehearsed weekly at Gateway School and were able to present a remarkably exciting and demanding series of performances during the decade, including Vivaldi's 'Gloria' and Ireland's 'These Things Shall Be', Britten's 'St Nicholas', Brahms' 'A Song of Destiny' and Vaughan Williams' 'Five Mystical Songs'.

Brass Bands

The English brass band movement is more commonly associated with the mills and the coal mines of Yorkshire and Lancashire, but Leicestershire has an equally strong tradition that is arguably more diverse than in the northern counties. Over many decades Leicestershire's bands have been supported not only by the collieries and by heavy industry, but also by a loosely related and sometimes uneasy grouping of organisations that included the Temperance Movement, friendly societies, independent chapels, working men's clubs and working-class political parties. In Leicestershire, alongside the Desford Colliery Band could be found the Wigston Temperance Band, the Coalville Ebenezer, the Ancient Order of Foresters and the City of Leicester Club and Institute.

Foresters Brass 2000, for example, began life in Leicester as the Bread Street Mission Band. Bread Street ran adjacent to Charles Street on the site of the present Haymarket Shopping Centre. In its time, the band has been known as the Leicester Ivanhoe Band, the North Evington Working Men's Club and Institute Band, the 1st Battalion Home Guard Band and the City of Leicester Special Constabulary Band. Throughout the 1960s, this long-established ensemble was known as the Leicester Foresters Band and was conducted by Ted Massey. Other Leicester bands have a similar history; the City of Leicester Band as it was known in the 1960s has also played as the Everards Brewery Band, the Bond Street Working Men's Club Band, the Bond Street Imperial Silver Band and the Leicester Club and Institute Band.

In the 1960s, as the coal industry began to face the challenge of alternative sources of power, its previous support for bands began to wane, following a pattern that had begun with the nationalisation of the industry in 1946. Bands looked wider for funding and began to gain sponsorship from diverse sources including retailers and building companies. This trend began in the 1960s and has continued to the present day, prompting subtle changes in the repertoire of bands. In the 1960s, there was a general move away from the traditional brass band repertoire towards lighter and more 'novelty' pieces in a sometimes misguided attempt to appeal to a wider audience and thus satisfy the marketing demands of the sponsors.

In Leicestershire there was a sometimes uneasy relationship between the world of the brass bands and the formal music training provided by Leicestershire County Council, and delivered through music teachers in schools. Some bands claimed that young people, whom they had introduced to music and trained, were being attracted away from the movement by their schools. However, there were instances when a talented young musician was able to embrace both worlds. Professor James Watson was a distinguished trumpet player and teacher who played with the Royal Philharmonic Orchestra, Paul McCartney and the Black Dyke Mills Band, among many other diverse ensembles and musicians. He became Professor of Trumpet at the Royal Academy of Music, began his musical career in the 1960s in the Desford Colliery Band (where he became principal cornet at just eleven years of age) and then the Leicestershire Schools Symphony Orchestra.

4

ENTERTAINMENT

The only challenge in the preceding decades to Leicester's theatres, music halls and picture houses was the wireless set, and possibly the weather. This was to change with breathtaking speed during the 1960s. With the possible exception of the first decade of the twenty-first century, at no other time has the way in which we have been entertained changed so dramatically. With these changes came a new social awareness and outlook on life.

The familiar wireless in its bulky Bakelite box, and with its valves and its illuminated dials listing a range of European radio stations, would give way to the slim portable transistor radio. The black-and-white images of the BBC and ITV (known as the Independent Television authority) would give way to colour and a new BBC channel in 1964. By the end of the decade, we were watching live images from the moon.

By comparison, public entertainment in Leicester was in a state of imbalance. Several of the old neighbourhood cinemas had closed, while those in the city centre needed to invest in order to keep ahead of the developing projection technology. Most significant was the fact that the city was without any professional theatre.

Clubs, Pubs and Coffee Bars

Although the De Montfort Hall and the Granby Halls both paid host to the most popular artists of the decade, many of the now iconic bands of the era could be heard at a number of smaller venues across the city. The Who, The Yardbirds and the Animals all played at Il Rondo (now Prezzo) in Silver Street, the top music venue of the period. Other venues included the Blue Beat Club in Conduit Street and coffee bars such as the Chameleon which stayed open much later than the public houses.

Compared with other cities in the Midlands, Leicester in the 1960s was regarded as a rather 'dead' place for night life. The principal club and dance hall in Leicester was the Palais at the junction of Humberstone Gate and St James Street. It was here that Gerry Dorsey, aka Englebert Humperdinck, performed before becoming popular enough to grace the stage of the much larger De Montfort Hall. Teenagers of the time remember the Palais's Friday lunchtime sessions for fourteen to eighteen-year-olds as well as the Monday and Friday night sessions finishing at 11 p.m. The Friday lunchtime session also served the younger employees of the hosiery trade who traditionally had Friday afternoons off.

Other popular haunts included the Lancaster Hall, which was part of the Lancaster Road Fire Station, and the Embassy, which was above the Co-op on Uppingham Road near to Humberstone Park. Students at Leicester University were able to dance to sounds of The Animals, The Small Faces, The Jimi Hendrix Experience, The Who, The Move and Traffic and Cream.

The Lee Circle car park opened in December 1961, the oldest multi-storey car park in Europe, and nearby was the bowling abbey that later became the Fusion nightclub. The alley was famous for being the largest – in terms of the number of lanes – outside the USA. Its conversion to a nightclub caused the construction of a sloping dance floor, which caused some problems for dancers who had imbibed one too many drinks! In April 1967, opposite the Abbey Motor Hotel in Abbey Street, Leicester's first nightclub opened. It was to be called the Penny Farthing and promised a late-night sophisticated, relaxed facility where customers could dance, wine and dine and socialise.

Television

Television in the 1960s changed from being an occasional form of entertainment in the corner of the living room to being an essential form of communication. In 1960, there were only two television channels, BBC and ITV, and both were in black and white. ITV led in terms of audience figures with a mass-market output that seemed brighter and more appealing than the comparatively dour BBC programmes. Viewing was limited to the late-afternoon and evening, with no service during the day except for a minority of schools programmes.

The top ten television programmes in January 1960 were all produced by ITV. These included *Emergency Ward Ten*, *Take Your Pick*, *No Hiding Place* and *Sunday Night at the London Palladium*. Significantly, a not dissimilar line-up featured as the most popular shows in the final month of the decade with the top slots occupied by *Coronation Street, This is Your Life, Special Branch,* and *News at Ten*, still all produced by ITV.

The launch of the American Telstar satellite on 11 July 1962 changed television overnight. This small piece of technology could beam television signals through space and across the world. A year later, British television audiences heard of the assassination of President John F. Kennedy by this means. It was a stimulus to much-needed further technical advances that were to improve picture definition and sound quality, and reduce the weight and the cost of television receivers. In just four years it was possible to watch programmes in colour.

A third television channel was launched by the BBC in April 1964. BBC Two was available only to viewers who had receivers with 625-line capability. As with many other advances in broadcast media, the subtle link between the broadcasters, the audience and the technology came into play. A wider choice of programmes produced a demand for better technology, which promoted a positive response from the manufacturers. 625-line technology enabled the development of colour transmissions. A limited service of certain colour programmes began on 1 July 1967, and by the end of that year the BBC was providing an almost full service with 80 per cent of its output in colour, including its transmissions from the transmitters serving Leicestershire and the other Midlands counties. At the end of the decade there were still only about 200,000 colour sets in Britain, but most programmes were being made in colour.

There were also many artistic milestones and significant programming moments on television during the 1960s. In December 1960, Granada Television in Manchester broadcast the first episode of *Coronation Street*. The BBC launched *Dr Who* on 23 November 1963 with the first appearance of the very durable Daleks, created by Terry Nation, just a few episodes later. The BBC's fight back against the dominance of

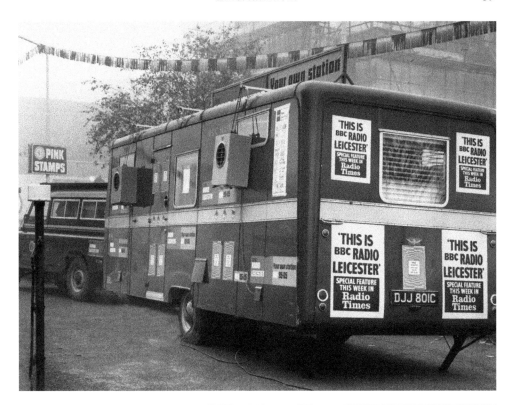

Above: A BBC outside broadcast unit parked in Lee Circle, prior to visiting the City of Leicester Show in Abbey Park in August 1967.

Right: BBC Radio Leicester staff interviewing workers at a manufacturing plant in Leicester in 1969.

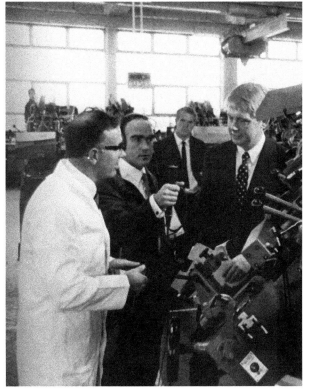

ITV included gritty drama and comedy including *Z Cars, Till Death Us Do Part, The Likely Lads,* as well as satire in the form of a sequence of cutting-edge programmes fronted by David Frost, beginning with *That Was the Week That Was.* Identifying a need to attract younger viewers, *Top of the Pops* was launched in January 1964. Although the transistor radio had brought portability to that medium, enabling young people to listen to their music away from the family group, the bulky and expensive television receiver was normally located in the family's living room, and it was usually father who decided what the family was to watch of an evening. It is estimated that 30 million people in the UK watched the 1966 World Cup final. The BBC claimed that 76 per cent of that audience watched its coverage of the game. The sometimes stormy relationship between football and sport would develop, generating very large television audiences and also very significant financial rewards for the top clubs and their players.

Television puppetry, which had begun in the 1950s with *Watch with Mother*, was developed into a range of programmes that are still respected today for their imaginative storylines and production techniques. Gerry Anderson and his pioneering 'Supermarionation' was first used with *Four Feather Falls*, which was first broadcast on 25 February 1960. Children went on to enjoy Anderson's other outputs, including *Supercar* (1961), *Fireball XL5* (1962), *Stingray* (1964/65) and *Thunderbirds* (1964–66).

The expansion of television in the 1960s was funded largely by considerable increases in the cost of the radio and television licences. In 1960, the TV cost £3 plus £1 excise duty. The radio-only licence cost £1. By the end of the decade, the TV licence had risen to £6, and £11 for colour. This equates to about £160 at 2014 prices. Over the same period, the number of TV licences issued increased by 33 per cent from 10.4 million to 15.6 million.

Radio

In 1948, the Copenhagen Plan had awarded a greater number of radio frequencies to the United Kingdom than to many other countries in Europe. As a result, the BBC, as the country's sole provider of radio programming, was technically free to expand. Paradoxically, because defeated Germany had been allocated very few frequencies, the country investigated VHF transmissions that were not covered by the plan. It was only at the end of the 1960s that the BBC began their VHF broadcasts. VHF (frequency modulated) transmissions were to become the mainstay of British radio broadcasting until Digital Audio Broadcasting (DAB) began in the early years of the twenty-first century.

Radio in 1960 was very similar to the post-war pattern of the Home Service, the Light Programme and the Third Programme, which on certain hours of the day became Network Three. This pattern, which had developed over the past thirty years, was to change in 1967 as a result of the BBC's 'Broadcasting in the Seventies' plan.

The plan was a somewhat belated response to the challenge from Radio Luxembourg and the pirate radio stations that had become established off the coast of England during the middle years of the decade. Radio Luxembourg, the only commercial radio station that could be heard in England, had recommenced broadcasting after the war on the very accessible 208 metres medium wave, playing music that the BBC was still hesitant to broadcast. Then pirate radio arrived, initially in the form of Radio Caroline, on two ships located off the Isle of Man and off the Essex coast, and Radio London broadcasting from the MV Galaxy, also off the Essex coast. By 1967, ten pirate radio stations were broadcasting to an estimated daily audience of 10–15 million.

The pirates satisfied a growing demand for the new music culture of the period that the BBC refused to acknowledge. The BBC's reluctance was partly due to the nature of the culture that this new music was perceived to reflect. In reality, it had no one on its staff who could relate to the music or to the listeners.

The BBC's response, when it came, was the 'Broadcasting in the Seventies' plan. The existing Light Programme, Home Service and Third Programme became Radio 2, Radio 3 and Radio 4. A brand new service – Radio 1 – was created, harnessing the energies and popularity of many of the former pirate radio presenters who had found themselves without work due to the government's Marine Offences Bill. Radio 1 began on 30 September 1967. The golden age of the pirate stations ended on the night of 2 March 1968 when the two Radio Caroline vessels were boarded and went off-air.

In Leicester, another element of the 'Broadcasting in the Seventies' plan moved in to an office block in Charles Street in 1967. Leicester was to be the home of Britain's first mainland local radio station. On 8 September 1967, BBC Radio Leicester began broadcasting a unique pattern of radio programming.

From the first day, it was obvious the sound of the new station was not targeting the young people of the city. The style of the presenters, who were mainly imported from the south of England, and the choice of music – mainly dance band and reflecting the popular trends of the past rather than the present – established a trend that became an entrenched statistic. BBC local radio, despite several attempts over the ensuing decades to reposition, still appeals mainly to an audience over the age of fifty years.

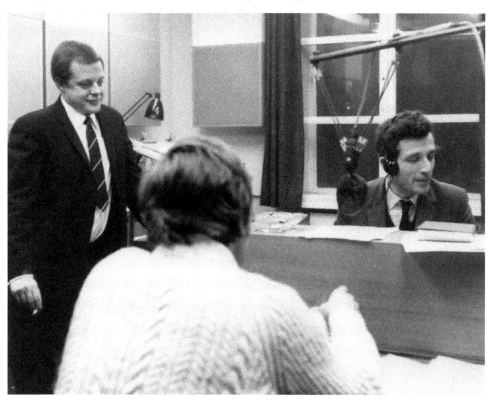

BBC Radio Leicester studios in 1967. At the control desk is Michael Murray, the first voice on the air in Leicester. Standing (*left*) is his colleague Dave Challis.

What sort of programmes are we going to hear?

News will be one of the main themes of the station. News of what's happened, happening and about to happen. News of people, places and events.

There will, of course, be many of the most popular programmes from the National networks, including the new popular music shows from Radio 1.

What about particular interests?

Gardening, civic affairs, industry, the churches and careers—all will have their own special programme.

What about women's programmes?

Women listeners will get their own feature every weekday morning covering fashions, shopping, home hints, etc. and there'll be special record request programmes for them. There'll also be request shows for hospital patients, children and old people.

What else will Radio Leicester have to offer?

Local weather forecasts . . . police and traffic information . . . sports results . . . personal interviews . . . radio car on the spot reports . . .

A BBC Radio Leicester publicity leaflet from 1967. Curiously, although 'news' was promised as a main theme, a newsroom was not set up until 1969.

However, BBC Radio Leicester strongly influenced the way Leicester people thought about their city and the way it was managed by politicians. For the first time the citizens of Leicester could hear their councillors and MPs, and could connect with them and the men and women who provided all the local, essential services. In the past, the only means by which the views of a politician or a manager of a utility could be received was through the columns of the *Leicester Mercury* or the *Leicester Evening Mail*. Now, for the first time, they could be heard. At first, technical issues prevented listeners from talking back to those whom they heard on air, but with the invention of the 'phone-in', a new era in local democracy was born.

BBC Radio Leicester also made local people more aware of their social environment. The hourly news bulletins were a compilation of stories about their neighbourhood and community. On Saturday afternoons, they heard live reports from Filbert Street and Welford Road, and in all the local programmes they heard Leicester people with Leicester accents. In its promotional material echoed in its pre-launch on-air trailers, the station described itself as 'the sound of Leicester'.

Formerly a reporter for the *Melton Times* in Leicestershire, the station's first manager was Maurice Ennals. He and his small team faced powerful opposition from the local newspapers, who feared that local news from the BBC would damage their circulation. He also faced internal challenges from other sectors of the BBC who did not support the idea of local radio. With remarkable energy and conviction, he contacted and consulted with individuals from every area of the local community, while fending off the public criticism, training his team and managing the construction of a complete radio station from scratch on the eighth floor of a city centre office block.

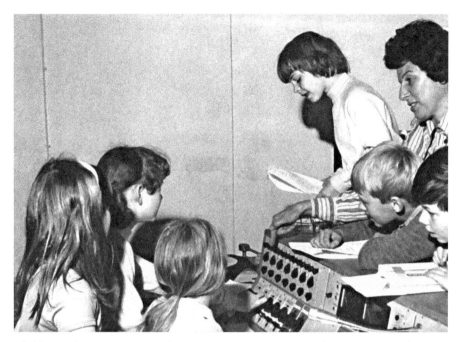

Children taking part in recording a programme at BBC Radio Leicester's Education Studio in Welford Road in 1968.

It is largely due to Ennal's shrewd and energetic project management that the station opened on time at 12.45 p.m. on 8 November 1967, and that two years later, the station, along with the other seven pilot operations, was deemed a success, leading to the extension of the fledging network across the country.

A meeting in a morgue between the BBC and the then leader of Leicester's Conservative group set the seal on plans for a local radio station in the city and gave Maurice Ennals, a founding father of the concept of local broadcasting, the opportunity to rewrite the motto of the BBC as 'Neighbour shall speak peace onto neighbour'. It was not until December 1966 that the BBC was granted permission to run a two-year experiment with eight local radio stations in England, and it was on 7 March 1967 that the then postmaster general, Edward Short, announced the names of the first three BBC local stations, one of which was Leicester.

In the elections of 1967, political control of the Corporation in Leicester changed, and the Conservatives indicated that they would not see through Labour's previous plans to provide funding for an experimental BBC station in the city. The meeting was brokered by Roland Orton, who was head of the Leicester News Service, which already provided the BBC Home Service in Birmingham with news from Leicester and took place in the BBC Studio on Freeman's Common, the former city morgue.

Although BBC Local Radio has always had its detractors and critics, and has faced severe financial restraints and the threat of extinction on several occasions, the stations continue to attract substantial audiences. Despite the many alternative sources for music, news and entertainment available through the internet, with instant access to information through social media, and the ability to download instantly music of every style and genre, BBC Radio Leicester is heard at some time each week by nearly a quarter of all adults in its transmission area.

Initially, it was thought that the potential local radio audience was limited because the station broadcast only on 95.05 VHF. VHF radio receivers were expensive, although several retailers in Leicester reported that they had sold out of their stocks prior to the station's launch. However, the new BBC Radio 1 achieved very high audiences from the first day at 247 metres on the medium wave, not far away on the dial from the well-known 208 metres location of Radio Luxembourg. Also, the national station's sound was familiar from the start, with presenters that teenagers already knew through the pirate radio stations, playing the music that teenagers wanted to hear.

An imaginative and mutually beneficial arrangement between the BBC and the Leicester Rediffusion Service, based nearby in Malabar Road formerly Dysart Street, gave both services an immediate boost. The Rediffusion system provided television and radio channels by wire to many thousands of homes in the new housing estates surrounding the city. The BBC agreed to feed BBC Radio 1 to Rediffusion in return for the company carrying BBC Radio Leicester's programmes when they were on the air. Initially, the radio station broadcast for as little as four hours a day, which enabled Rediffusion's customers to hear BBC Radio 1 for many hours of the day. In addition, the continuity presenters on Radio Leicester provided frequent references to the 'listeners on Rediffusion Channel D'.

At first, BBC Radio Leicester was described as an 'experiment', thus affording the BBC the option of abandoning the project if the station in Leicester and the other seven local stations across England failed to attract listeners. BBC Radio Leicester's first major challenge came in September 1968, when exceptionally heavy thunderstorms and rainfall brought flooding to Leicester's suburbs. Although the

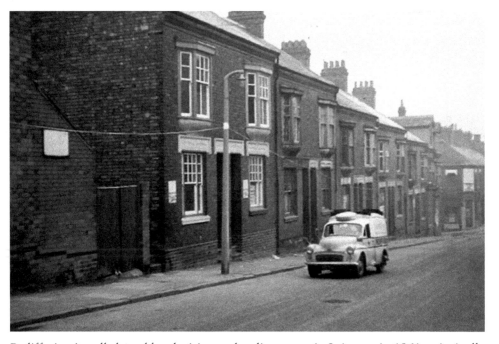

Rediffusion installed a cable television and radio system in Leicester in 1961, principally serving the housing estates. In this photograph, an engineer is at work on overhead cables in the Highfields area. The Morris Minor 'cables' van is on Upper Kent Street directly opposite the junction with Garendon Street. This section of Upper Kent Street is now Maidstone Road.

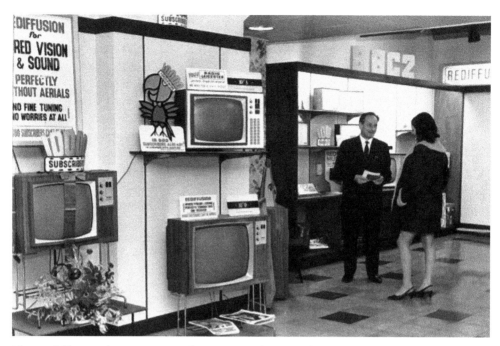

The Rediffusion showroom in Belvoir Street photographed in 1968. Rediffusion received transmissions from a mast situated in Western Park. Their technical headquarters were in Malabar Road, St Matthew's Estate.

station had no newsroom, it succeeded in broadcasting live accounts of the conditions, even resorting to transmitting from a rowing boat floating in the flood waters in Saffron Lane.

Cinema

One of the many simple but useful services that BBC Radio Leicester offered was a daily list of the films being screened in local cinemas. However, by that time in the last years of the decade, the list was dwindling. The decline in ticket sales that had begun after the war with the reopening of the television service continued. It was the death knell for the local neighbourhood cinemas. The Tudor in Tudor Road closed in 1958. The Sovereign in Woodgate closed in 1961. The Trocadero, Uppingham Road, was converted to a bingo hall in 1963 and was burnt down in 1967.

In the city centre, five cinemas were open for business for most of the 1960s. The largest were the ABC (formerly the Savoy) in Belgrave Gate and the Odeon in Queen Street. The ABC was later converted to three screens and renamed the Cannon; the Odeon could seat 2,183 customers. The Gaumont in the marketplace was still known at the time, by the older generation, as the City Cinema. It was later to become another Odeon. The Cameo in High Street bucked the trend by reopening in the 1960s, having operated previously as the Electric Theatre, the Imperial Playhouse and the Arcadia. A new small cinema was built in 1965 on the ground floor of the Abbey Street multi-storey development that included the Abbey Motor Hotel. In the outlying neighbourhoods, the Evington Cinema in East Park Road and the Fosse on Fosse Road North also remained open for business.

As with the other forms of entertainment, British cinema changed significantly during the 1960s, following the revolution in music, fashion and social attitudes, but the most popular films were the musicals that were suitable for a family audience and included *My Fair Lady* (1964), *Mary Poppins* (1964), *The Sound of Music* (1965) and *Oliver!* (1968). *Lawrence of Arabia* (1962) was another landmark film of the period, as was David Lean's epic, *Dr Zhivago* (1965).

Hammer Productions continued to produce their own unique contribution to the film industry with a sequence of Frankenstein and Dracula films, as well as two 'mummy' movies, and arguably their most well-known film *One Million Years BC* in 1966, starring Raquel Welch. In all, Hammer released twenty-eight films during the decade.

A new, more challenging and controversial form of cinema began with *Saturday Night and Sunday Morning* directed by Karel Reisz, and released in 1960, which focused on working-class issues in an open and frank style. *A Kind of Loving* directed by John Schlesinger in 1962, *The Loneliness of the Long Distance Runner* by Tony Richardson in 1962, *Billy Liar* also by Schlesinger in 1963, and Lindsay Anderson's *This Sporting Life* (1963) created controversy and debate as much as they provided entertainment. Also demanding and challenging in the latter half of the decade were *The Graduate* (1967), *Who's Afraid of Virginia Woolf?* (1966) and *The Swimmer* (1968), starring Burt Lancaster. By 1969, Leicester audiences were viewing the immensely controversial dramatisation by Ken Russell of D. H. Lawrence's *Women in Love*. With such daring directors and provocative material, the stage – or rather the big screen – was set for release of the one of the most notorious films of all time, Stanley Kubrick's *A Clockwork Orange* in December 1971.

Despite improvements in cinema technology, wide screen and stereo sound, and the blockbusters that earned many millions of pounds for the studios and distributors, ticket sales at cinemas across the UK fell by almost 50 per cent between 1961 and 1970.

Theatre

Although the splendid Little Theatre in Dover Street was providing good entertainment and well-produced shows, with the closure of all of Leicester's traditional and long-standing theatres the city was without a purpose-built venue for professional theatre in the 1960s. The Theatre Royal had closed its doors after the 1952/53 season. The last performance at the Palace Theatre had been on 11 February 1959 and at the Opera House on 11 June 1960. It was not until 1973 that a new theatre would be constructed as part of the new Haymarket Shopping Centre, directly opposite where the former Palace Theatre has stood for so many years.

As a temporary solution to the lack of a venue, Leicester City Council announced in 1963 that it would build a theatre which would be inexpensive to construct but would be capable of staging quality productions. The site that was selected had limited potential for development because of its location between Newarke Street and Upper Brown Street. It was designed by the council's architect department and completed in six months, and based on a similar plan to the Mermaid Theatre in Puddle Dock in London. It was called, appropriately, the Phoenix Theatre. From the outset, the council regarded it as a temporary venue with a life expectancy of ten years. It cost just £21,175 to build, compared with the Nottingham Playhouse which cost £375,000, and less than £4,000 to equip. Compared with the old Leicester theatres, the Phoenix was small with just 274 seats in a tiered auditorium, but because all the seats had the same unobstructed view of the stage, and the seating was relatively comfortable, the theatre had an intimacy and immediate appeal. The first performance took place on 8 October 1963 being *The Matchmaker* by Thornton Wilder, and starring Thelma Ruby.

Throughout the 1960s the Phoenix achieved considerable artistic and commercial success under its director, Colin Midgley. Famous names to grace the stage included Richard Eyre and Anthony Hopkins in his first professional role, Richard Briers, and Miriam Margolyes. Guest directors included Michael Bogdanov and Clive Perry. Leicester author Sue Townsend became closely associated with the Phoenix; her play *Captain Christmas and the Evil Adults* was in production at the theatre in 1963.

In 1960 Leicester City Council and the theatre committee encouraged a group of actors to set up the *Living Theatre* in the old St Nicholas School Rooms. These were situated between Holy Bones and Great Central Street in Leicester, and were scheduled for demolition in July 1961 as part of the Central Ring, Southgates Underpass and St Nicholas Circle development scheme. The theatre had an open-end stage and the walls of the auditorium were painted black to enable the audience of 200 to concentrate on the stage area.

The group of actors contributed their savings to fund the project. They were led by Bill Hays, Derrick Goodwin and Brian Grellis, with such significant figures as Jill Gascoine, Kenneth Colley, Peter Blythe and Ken Loach as members. Kenneth Colley, famous in more recent times for his appearances in *Star Wars*, left his job as an assistant stage manager for a repertory theatre company in Kent to work in Leicester. Jill Gascoine had previously collaborated with Ken Loach at the Dundee Repertory theatre. The opening production was *Trials* by Christopher Logue. Other productions were presented on a fortnightly basis and included *Roots, Chips with Everything, Luther*, and *The Knack*. The demolition was later than planned, which allowed the company to continue until January 1963. Their final production was *Billy Liar* on the 12 January 1963.

The Little Theatre enjoyed a membership of over 1,000 members in the 1960s and maintained its busy output throughout the decade, with a different production every

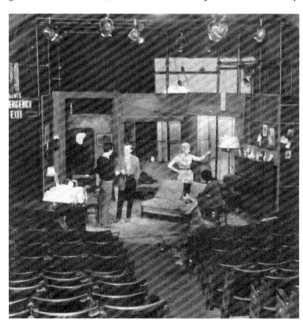

The Living Theatre Group working in the St Nicholas School Hall (1961–63) after all other theatres in Leicester had closed.

month except in August. Musical comedy, opera and operetta were also presented on the Little Theatre's stage by local societies who hired the theatre on a regular basis.

The Phoenix remained Leicester's Repertory Theatre with a youthful and energetic resident company until 1973 and the opening of the new Haymarket Theatre. The name lives on in the form of the Phoenix Square independent cinema and digital gallery near to Leicester's newest theatre, Curve. The building is still in use as a performance centre supported by De Montfort University and Leicester College.

The De Montfort Hall

For more than a century, in which the nature of entertainment and the demands and expectations of the audiences have changed considerably, one venue has remained consistently relevant, respected and valued. Leicester's De Montfort Hall, designed and built by local architect Shirley Harrison, opened in 1913 at a cost of £21,000, but even in the twenty-first century it is a stylish building that still looks fresh and pleasing to the eye. It is also a very successful performance venue and still the largest venue in the city.

In the 1960s, the De Montfort Hall played host to the top names in entertainment and pop music. The Beatles played here twice in 1963 and returned in 1964. In common with all their gigs in that year, the band played ten songs, including 'From Me to You', 'I Saw Her Standing There', 'All My Loving', 'She Loves You' and 'Twist and Shout'. On the same bill were Tommy Roe and Chris Montez. For their two appearances in one day on Saturday 10 October 1964, John, Paul, George and Ringo were paid the princely sum of £850. Dusty Springfield also sang on stage twice in 1963 and again in 1964. The Rolling Stones rocked the hall with no less than three appearances in 1965, and Status Quo's appearance in 1968 is still remembered by their many fans.

In 1960 Judy Garland sang to a packed house at the De Montfort Hall. It was significant for the gay community in the Leicester area, which largely remained hidden and unseen. One member of the audience wrote later of the experience, in a letter to author and researcher Richard Dyer:

> I shall never forget walking into the De Montfort Hall. Our seats were very near the front and we had to walk all the way down the centre gangway of a hall already crowded. I think every queen in the East Midlands catchment area had made it ... Everyone had put on their Sunday best, had haircuts and had bought new ties. There was an exuberance, a liveliness, a community of feeling which was quite new to me and probably quite rare anyway then. It was as if the fact that we had gathered to see Garland gave us permission to be gay in public for once.

Perhaps the secret to the continuing success of the De Montfort Hall has been its ability, partly due to its design, to cater for any form of public entertainment. Throughout the 1960s and in other decades, it was a familiar venue for classical music lovers, theatre-goers, evangelistic religious groups, wrestling fans, parents of children in city and county school orchestras, those who enjoyed stand-up comedians, followers of amateur brass bands, organ enthusiasts and the young fans of bands such as The Beatles and The Rolling Stones. There was also an enlightened management in the form of a city entertainments manager who had the freedom to decide on the type of artist, act and event that would work for the venue.

5

LEISURE

Leisure in the 1960s, as a specific activity to which an individual or a family devoted a specific time, was not such a well-defined concept as it is in the twenty-first century. Most working-class men were at their place of work between 9 a.m. and 5 p.m., and families employed in the textile, hosiery and knitwear trades were working shift patterns. Of necessity, leisure time was more often spent relaxing at home for an evening or going to a football match on a Saturday afternoon.

Organised fitness and leisure was still to come to Leicester, with the exception of boxing clubs, but for those who sought exercise there were the parks and the new swimming baths. For those who wanted more mental stimulus, the city provided museums and libraries, though these seemed less enticing to children and young people who were becoming used to learning through the medium of television.

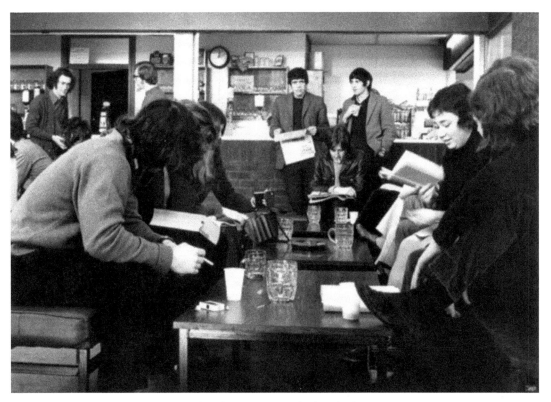

The students' bar at Leicester Polytechnic photographed in the late 1960s.

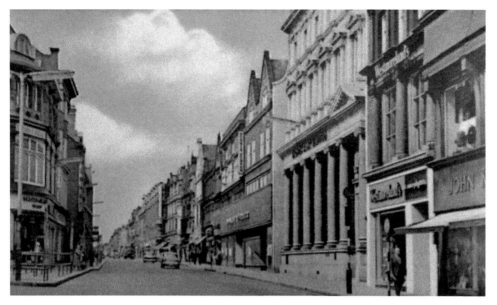

The High Street from the clock tower. This artist's impression dates to the early 1960s, and highlights the elegance of the Victorian and Edwardian frontages – and a lack of traffic.

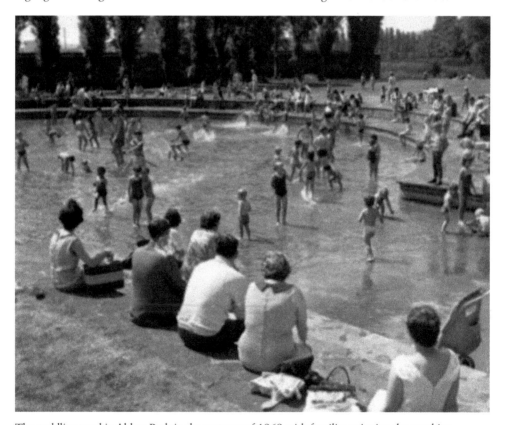

The paddling pool in Abbey Park in the summer of 1969 with families enjoying the sunshine.

Parks

The 57 acres of Abbey Park has been a favourite recreational area for the people of Leicester since it was laid out between 1879 and 1882. The land north-west of the river was added in 1932. It was an imaginative scheme to improve the city's flood defences, and used the soil excavated from the widened river and the artificial lake to create mounds on which over 30,000 trees were planted.

In the 1960s, Abbey Park and the other major open spaces in the city – Victoria Park, Western Park and those in the suburbs – were all in regular use. In a period of relative prosperity, parks were well maintained with an adequate workforce to manage the mowing of the grass, care of the woodlands and the planting of flower borders. There were less safety concerns. Children's play equipment was fairly unimaginative, but potentially dangerous with the risk of trapped fingers and broken limbs, and if a child fell from a swing they would land on hard concrete or paving, rather than the soft surfaces which were developed in later decades.

There were fewer litter bins in Leicester's parks. Although the era of disposable containers had arrived, there was generally less litter. Dog bins were not yet being deployed, but there was a workforce available to clean up behind the parks' visitors at regular intervals.

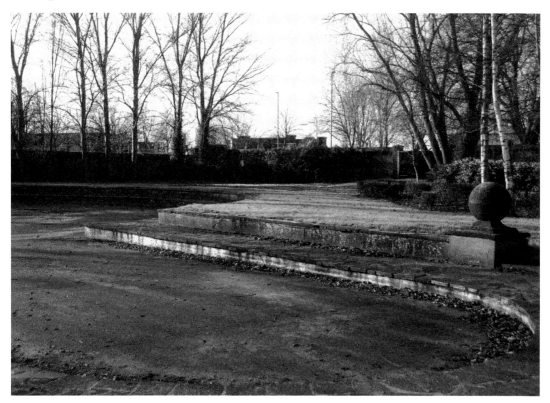

The Abbey Park paddling pool in January 2015. The surrounding play area has been extensively modernised, and in 2015 Leicester City Council proposed reopening the pool if modern safety and hygiene standards could be met.

The City of Leicester Show

For many Leicester families, the highlight of the year, apart from the Industrial Fortnight in July, was the annual City of Leicester Show, held in Abbey Park on the late summer bank holiday and the following day. The event evolved from the earlier annual flower shows that had been staged in the park since the 1940s, and which for some years incorporated a swimming gala.

By the 1960s, the show involved many different elements of entertainment, a funfair and a strong commercial presence. The horticultural element remained at its heart with large marquees housing competitive displays of flowers, fruit and vegetables, reflecting the park's other role in Victorian times as a landscape in which plants could be cultivated and displayed to their best advantage. In earlier times, Abbey Park's collection of Echeverias and its Chrysanthemum House gained a national reputation.

As this was the major public event in Leicester, attracting tens of thousands of people, the City of Leicester Show was the obvious place in which the BBC could launch the main publicity drive for its new local radio station. Consequently, an outside broadcast unit arrived for the show in August 1967, nine weeks before the station was due to go on air. The small team of producers also used the occasion to recruit freelance contributors, notably Geoff Amos, a local gardening expert who was present at the show to judge the Chrysanthemum entries. He was invited to present a regular gardening feature, which began during Radio Leicester's first week of programmes and developed into *Down to Earth*, which had been broadcast regularly and without a break ever since.

Attendance at the show held steady throughout the 1960s and the following decade, but then began to decline. The cost of staging the event began to increase year on year which led to a reduction in the quality of the special attractions paid for by the council. Eventually, in 1995, the event was abandoned.

Allotments

The expanding urban environment following the Industrial Revolution, when those who lived and worked in the cities became more and more displaced from the open countryside, led to the creation of allotments. It became a legal requirement of local authorities to provide land for allotments in 1908. Several of Leicester's allotments date from this early period, including the Belgrave Allotment Society, which was founded one year after the legislation reached the statute books.

The concept of growing your own vegetables had been encouraged during the war when every available space across the city, including some school playing fields and parkland, had been turned into allotments. However, from the mid-1950s, the demand for land to be used for housing and industrial uses led to many requests for land to be handed over by the allotment societies for development. The greater affluence also meant that fresh produce was readily available in shops, which led many people to stop growing their own and to allotment plots being left unused and neglected.

In the 1960s, allotments were more popular with the older generation. The Soil Association had been founded in 1946 and the Henry Doubleday Research Association in 1954, but despite their activities as yet there was little awareness of environmental issues such as the packaging of vegetables and the use of fertilisers which had been actively encouraged as early as the 1947 Agriculture Act. Concepts such as self-sufficiency were considered only by a small minority of people. Although children would help their fathers on their allotment plot, few young families would choose to apply for an allotment until it became a 'trendy' idea in the 1970s, a concept and a way of life so perfectly reflected by the BBC comedy series *The Good Life*, which was broadcast from 1975 to 1978.

Toys, Books and Hobbies

A minor revolution in children's toys began at the beginning of 1958 with the patenting of the modern, plastic Lego brick. It marked not only the launch of one of the most successful and universal construction toys, but the beginning of a shift away from toys fabricated from wood, textiles and metal to injection-moulded plastic.

One of the first toy manufacturers to move to injection moulding was Palitoy, the Leicestershire company based in Coalville. Their range of toys available during the 1960s included Action Man, launched in 1966 and based on the successful American GI Joe; Tiny Tears, which was manufactured between 1950 and 1968; and Tressy, originally an American doll with hair that could grow, which was produced between 1963 and 1965.

Plastic construction kits such as Airfix were popular during the 1960s when children had longer periods of free time and were willing to concentrate on complex and detailed work. Space exploration began to catch the public imagination, with rockets and space ships joining jet aircraft as the popular models to build.

The development of radio equipment based on the transistor led to models that could be controlled remotely. The old Meccano construction kits, which had been powered by wind-up clockwork motors for many years, were still selling well, and could be easily updated. Hornby and Tri-ang model railway sets were still very popular with boys, as were the increasing range of Dinky Toys and those made by Corgi. Corgi switched from metal to plastic manufacture during this period, and released their first car with an opening feature – their Aston Martin DB4 with a hinged door – in February 1960. In 1964, Corgi's parent company, Mettoy, launched a range of smaller scale vehicles under the Husky brand, which were less expensive and designed to compete with Matchbox toys.

Serving the educational and instructional market, J. & L. Randall Ltd, a Hertfordshire-based company, manufactured a range of well-engineered stationery steam and electric motors designed to power other toys, and a set of student microscopes complete in a box with tweezers, slides and detailed instructions.

Another durable toy of the period was the toy typewriter manufactured by Petite. These were toys that worked and copied the typewriters that grown-ups used. There are so many examples from the 1960s that are still being sold and used today, that at least one manufacturer of typewriter ribbons is now producing a ribbon that can be used on Petite products. A toy with a similar concept was the child's sewing machine, with several different versions available, including at least one product by the famous Singer Sewing Machine Co.

Slot cars in the form of Scalextric had been launched at the Harrogate Toy Fair in 1957 and sold to Lines Brothers, the parent company of Tri-ang. This immensely popular toy began as a pressed metal product, but the change to plastic manufacture was made in the early 1960s. The first tracks were made from a rubberised compound but these were also later produced in plastic.

More gentle pursuits, which were often shared by children and adults, included building collections of postage stamps, coins and cigarette cards. For the girls, the age-old attraction of dolls, prams and doll's houses remained.

One unusual and transient craze was trolls. Also known in the UK as gonks, these were plastic dolls with furry hair. They had been launched in 1959 by Thomas Dam, a Danish fisherman and woodcutter who could not afford a Christmas gift for his young daughter, and carved the first troll doll from his imagination. The invention became one of the most popular toys in the UK and the USA during the 1960s, and trolls are still collected today. Original trolls are now valuable, and some enthusiasts have up to 1,500 trolls in their collection.

The traditional board games that had absorbed families for generations were still to be found in drawers and cupboards – Monopoly, ludo, snakes and ladders, draughts and Scrabble – but their popularity began to wane as television viewing increased. There had been some attempts to reinvigorate the market with games like Risk, a board game with the theme of political world dominance launched in 1959, but these never caught the imagination in the same way as the older games. By the end of the decade, the development of plastic manufacturing came to the boxed game in the form of Mastermind, invented by an Israeli postmaster, but manufactured in Leicester since 1971 by Invicta Plastics of Oadby and at the present time by Hasbro.

Almost every child in the UK used handicraft products made by the Leicester-based Dryad Handicrafts Co. in schools. During the First World War, the Dryad Works provided a Leicester hospital with off-cuts of cane for basket-making by wounded soldiers. Dryad Handicrafts was a response by the company's founder Harry Hardy Peach to a growing demand for cane and other craft materials for use in occupational therapy and in schools. Peach had set up his Dryad Cane Furniture Works in 1909. A farsighted and intelligent man of great integrity, he strove throughout his life to create mass-produced goods to the highest standards of design and to treat both his employees and his customers with respect. By the 1960s, Dryad was the largest supplier of handicraft projects in the world.

Children also continued to read books and comics during the 1960s, although television was beginning to be a temptation away from the printed word. As well as the classics, contemporary children's authors were publishing excellent material. Alan Garner's *The Owl Service*, published in 1967, is a fine example of books for the older child that were challenging as well as exciting.

From the USA came several authors writing for younger children who were developing their vocabulary. Theodor Seuss Geisel published over sixty children's books over the course of several decades under the pseudonym Dr Seuss. His bestselling books of the 1960s included *Green Eggs and Ham*, *Dr Suess's ABC*, *Fox in Socks*, and *The Sneetches and Other Stories*. His colleague P. D. Eastman also worked in the same field, and in this decade published *Are You My Mother?*, *Go, Dog, Go!* and *The Cat in the Hat Beginner Book Dictionary*.

Many children read comics, often delivered weekly to their homes with the newspaper and the *Radio Times*. The notorious stalwarts – *The Beano*, *The Dandy*, *The Topper* and *The Beezer* – remained popular throughout the decade. *Bunty*, for girls, had been launched by D. C. Thomson in 1958. There was also the *Eagle* comic, one of the most iconic of all British comics, founded in 1950 by Anglican vicar Revd Marcus Morris, who felt that the church was out of touch with children and young people and continued to sell well. *Girl*, also a creation of the Revd Morris, was published until October 1964 when it merged with *Princess*. Another popular comic from the Hulton Press as a companion to *Eagle*, *Girl* and *Swift*, and aimed at a very young readership, was *Robin* which continued to be published until 1969.

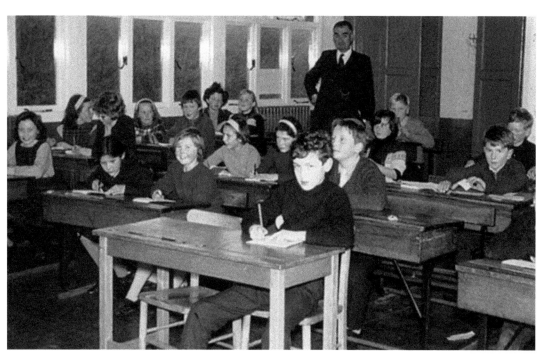

A typical primary school classroom in the early 1960s. This is Huncote Road School in Narborough.

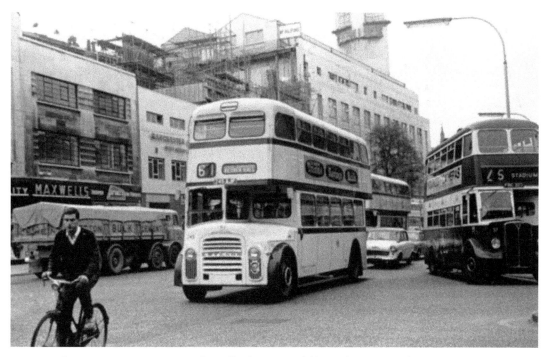

Humberstone Gate in 1965, with traffic, buses (in different liveries) and pedestrians. Lewis's department store predominates, and adjacent is the Manchester Club and Institute and Maxwells, a Leeds-based company selling gowns.

Libraries, Museums and Public Baths

The first public baths in Leicester to be provided by the governing authority of the town were built by the Romans. The remains were discovered by chance next to St Nicholas church when the corporation was investigating the suitability of the site for the construction of new baths.

The provision of public amenities began in the middle of the nineteenth century during a period of reform that began with the Parliamentary Reform Act of 1832 and the Factories Act in the following year. The 1845 Museums Act empowered local authorities to raise money through taxation to fund public museums. In 1846 the Public Baths and Wash Houses Act was approved by Parliament and this was followed in 1850 by the Public Libraries Act, which gave local authorities the powers to establish free library services.

The Victorian legacy was still very apparent in the 1960s, not only in Leicester but in most towns and cities in the UK. The majority of libraries and museums were housed in gaunt red-brick buildings, designed, like many schools, hospitals and pumping stations of the period, in Victorian Gothic style. The lofty ceilings, wide staircases and stained-glass windows were more in keeping with cathedrals than in municipal buildings that were intended to serve the public.

The concept of that time was to display artefacts and indicate their provenance, but not to provide explanation or interpretation. 'Do not touch' was the most frequently displayed sign. Although education in schools was changing, in the 1960s the contents

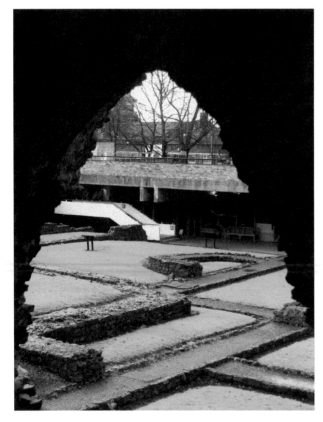

The Jewry Wall Museum and Vaughan College complex, combining the texture of the Roman remains with brutal concrete structures, was designed by Trevor Dannatt and completed in 1962.

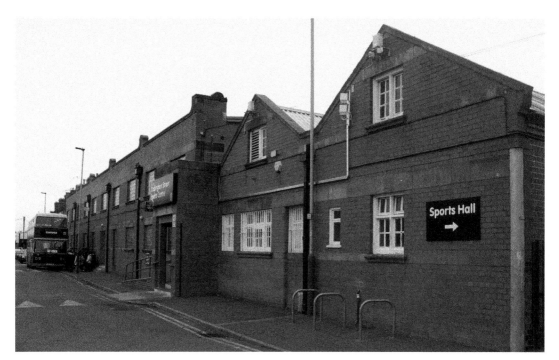

The Cossington Street Baths, although looking jaded and antiquated, are still serving their purpose as part of a wider recreation and community facility in the Belgrave area.

of most museums were behind wooden framed glass cabinets or chain barriers, and there was little understanding of the concept of social history.

In Leicester in 1962, by coincidence on the site of the Roman baths, the Jewry Wall Museum was constructed, which applied the latest concepts and ideas to the way a museum could be laid out. Visitors could relate to the modest proportions of the building, and the exhibits were no longer isolated from their context. Instead of a confusing array of items from different periods, here was an integrated collection with artefacts that related one to the other, and to real places familiar to the people who visited.

The proposed new public baths, which were planned for the site, were eventually built nearby on the opposite side of Highcross Street. St Margaret's Baths were designed by the city's architects' department and were opened on 11 February 1966 by Dennis Howell MP, later to become the Minister for Sport. Originally, it was planned that the baths would be part of a much larger integrated centre that would include a cinema, hotel and car park, and would connect to the shopping areas of the city by monorail. These ideas would have to wait until the construction of the Highcross Centre in the last years of the twentieth century. The monorail is still on the drawing board. However, the baths did not survive to see the completion of the grand idea. They were demolished in 2000.

6

THE URBAN LANDSCAPE

The Second World War had changed Leicester's urban landscape, but not to such an extent as in neighbouring Coventry, where wholesale reconstruction was necessary in the immediate post-war years. In Leicester some of the bomb sites remained to become unofficial car parks by the 1960s. It was the growth in population and the number of motor vehicles which brought about the massive building programmes that were to change the face of Leicester and its suburbs. It is a relationship that is still the focus of town and country planning in the twenty-first century. More houses prompted the need to encourage business and commerce in order to provide employment, and more roads to accommodate the increased traffic travelling between the home and the workplace.

Although Leicester had a development plan that looked forward a full fifty years, it was never completed, and various issues including lack of finance and changes in political policy locally and nationally resulted in schemes being amended and reduced in scale. The use of concrete changed the former red-brick harmony of the city into an uninviting grey landscape. The materials of the time and the theories resulted in a legacy that includes the depressing Southgates Underpass and St Nicholas Circle, which destroyed so much of Leicester's Roman and medieval archaeology.

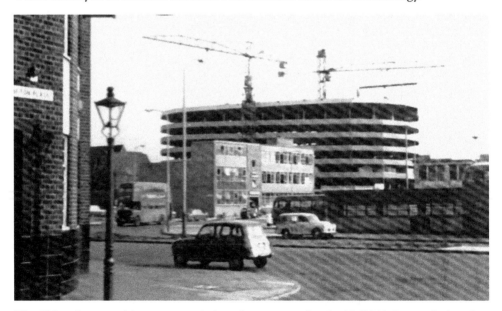

The Abbey Street multi-storey car park under construction in 1963/64. It was designed to accommodate a hotel on its upper floors with a supermarket, petrol station and restaurant.

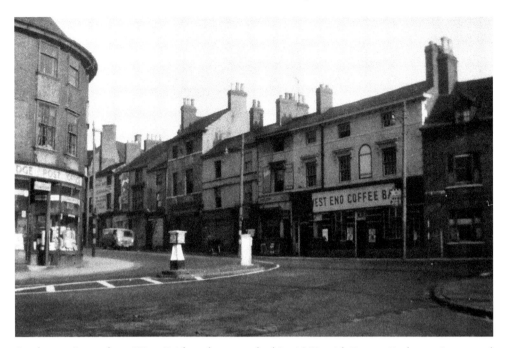

Applegate Street from West Bridge photographed in 1962 with Lower Redcross Street and Castle Street on the right. The West End Coffee Bar was formerly the Mitre and Keys Public House. This is now St Nicholas Circle where the Holiday Inn stands.

Housing

Although tracts of land in the Wharf Street area of Leicester had been subject to slum clearance in the immediate post-war years, lack of finance had brought the original plan to a halt. The city council believed that, among the many families who needed to be rehoused, there was a strong preference for houses with gardens rather than apartments of flats. However, the grants provided by central government were much greater for flats. Eventually, the council adopted a plan for a mix of housing while also providing space for industrial units. More than 200 business premises were demolished to make way for the clearance scheme and the new ring road.

In 1958 the council announced that the scheme would continue in order to address the number of families on the housing waiting list, which stood at around 12,000. This next stage, which extended the original clearance area further along Wharf Street, lacked a clear strategy, but nevertheless compulsory purchase orders were issued on properties in the network of streets between Belgrave Gate and Catherine Street in the area through which Dysart's Way now runs. In the final stage, 250 properties in Birstall Street, Syston Street, Curzon Street and Cobden Street were acquired for demolition in October 1962. A project that had taken twelve years to fulfil, the St Matthew's Estate was completed in 1966.

Throughout the decade the expansion of the city's housing stock continued. In 1966 20 acres of land was acquired near the General Hospital, on which the Rowlatts Hill Estate was constructed. Two years later, demolition began in the Sparkenhoe Street and Melbourne Road area of Highfields in readiness for what was to become the St Peter's Estate. This was an optimistic but ill-conceived plan undertaken by the council using Direct Labour, a decision that became a near-disaster. Structural problems were found

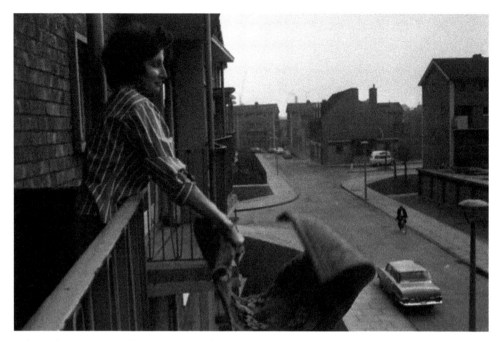

Life on the new St Matthew's Estate in the 1960s.

in the high-rise blocks, which led to all construction work in those areas being halted. Technical surveys resulted in the scheme being taken over by private contractors, and the design and height of the blocks being reduced. The four blocks that were finally built were not available for occupation until 1973.

Town Planning and Roads

It was in this decade that the city of Leicester became more closely linked with London and the southern counties of England following the completion of the M1 motorway through Leicestershire in 1965. Leicester's central location within the country and the expanding motorway network was to give the city a different form of commercial opportunity in the future – namely road haulage and distribution. The M1 was also to bring more people and more vehicles, and further focused the planners' minds in terms of how to deal with the steadily increasing traffic on Leicester's roads.

By 1960 Leicester's road map was already changing, but major changes were to take place over the following years. The first phases of the Central Ring, Burley's Way and Vaughan Way, from the junction with the Belgrave Road towards the south-west of the city, had already been opened, with a roundabout at its intersection with ancient Highcross Street. The continuation, necessitating the construction of the Southgates Underpass and St Nicholas Circle, was still only in the earliest of planning stages, so that network of little streets to the east of the West Bridge – Applegate Street, Thornton Lane, Harvey Lane and Redcross Street – was still in existence, although looking shabby and run down.

Linking Charles Street and Belgrave Gate, north of this area, was Bread Street, where the old Leicester City Transport central bus garage stood. This garage was a useful addition to the main bus depot on Abbey Park Road and accommodated spare buses that could be utilised at the busy lunch time and evening peak periods. The Bread Street premises and

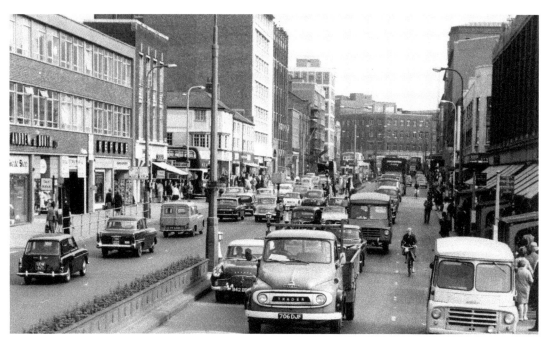

Charles Street looking south. The bus on the left is in Humberstone Gate travelling eastwards out of the city. A 'Beckett Bucket' (planter for flowers), which was a notable feature of Charles Street, is seen in the lower left-hand side of the photograph.

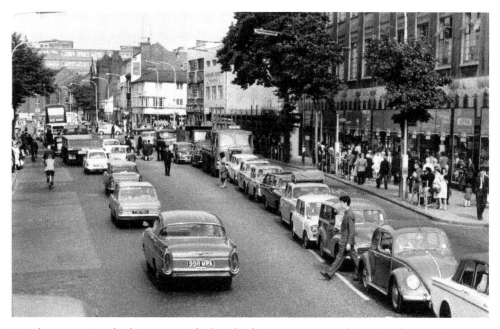

Humberstone Gate looking east with the Charles Street junction bisecting the two buses. On the right is Lewis's department store. The queue of traffic heading east is trailed by a classic American influenced Vauxhall Velox from about 1960, following a 1963 Vauxhall Viva. The wide expanse of Humberstone Gate is clear and eventually a central reservation was provided in order to give pedestrians a mid-point safe refuge.

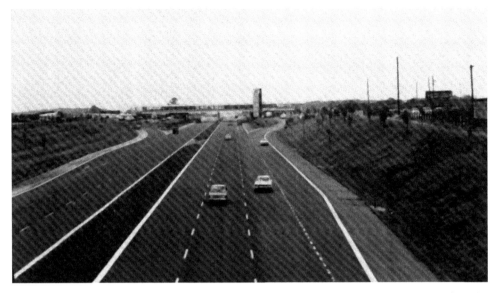

The construction of the M1 motorway through Leicestershire in 1965 (here viewed at the Leicester Forest East service station) signalled major social and economic changes for the city and county, and an emphasis on road rather than rail freight. Leicestershire is now a major national hub for transport logistics services. The service station could be demolished if proposals to improve the nearby intersection go ahead.

the adjacent Humberstone Gate facility in fact dated back to the tram era. Between the Bell Hotel and the Clock Tower on Humberstone Gate was a narrow lane known locally as 'the hole on the wall'. In former years, until 1949, the trams would use this route to the 'central depot'. The lane opened out into a larger forecourt that extended to Bread Street. Until the Haymarket Shopping Centre was built, buses required for rush hour-only duties were garaged here. Coincidentally, in 2015, Leicester City Council began work on a new bus station partly on the former route of Bread Street. The Bread Street Mission could also be found in the same vicinity.

Similarly, where the Highcross Shopping Centre now stands, the shops, workshops and other Victorian buildings in the shadow of High Street and Churchgate – St Peter's Lane, Union Street, West, North and East Bond Streets and Little Lane – could still be explored. The spine of the medieval town was still a route that could be taken by cars, from the Groby Road, south through Woodgate and Frog Island, Highcross Street and Southgates Street to Oxford Street.

In September 1962, Konrad Smigielski arrived in Leicester. He had been appointed to a new role as the chief planning officer for the city of Leicester. Leicester was only the second city in the country to make such an appointment. In the ten years (less four months) that he held the position (which ended in an agreement that he should seek early retirement), the landscape of Leicester changed dramatically, but not as extensively as he wished. Yet many of his seemingly controversial proposals were ideas that had been set out by his predecessor, John Beckett, and it was Smigielski who was able to provide a rationale for those plans. Although his eventual plan was called the Leicester Traffic Plan, Smigielski was not a slave to the internal combustion engine. He saw the way in which increasing prosperity was encouraging the sale of family cars, and he knew that at some time in the future the city would be overwhelmed unless steps

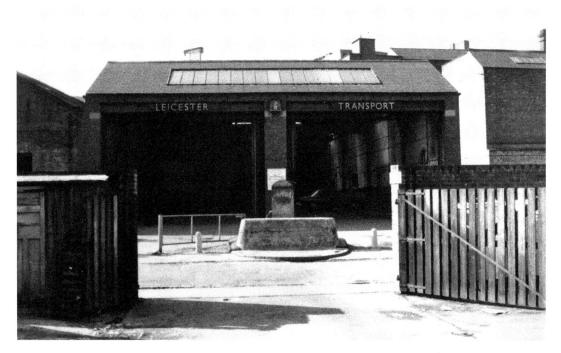

Above: The former Leicester Transport Garage in Bread Street, demolished to make way for the Haymarket Shopping Centre. Coincidentally, the later Charles Street bus terminus was constructed near to this location and was being rebuilt again in 2015.

Right: Gallowtree Gate in December 2014. Pedestrianised and spacious, but no elevated monorail as Smigielski had proposed.

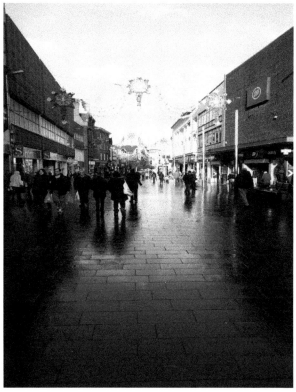

were taken. His philosophy was that 'it would be fundamentally wrong to plan cities for traffic only; they have to be planned for living.'

In a world where the inventions of science fiction writers were becoming a reality with men in space, and satellites were circling the earth transmitting television images across the world, the idea of a city linked by high-level passenger-carrying monorail systems did not seem too far-fetched. The well-travelled Smigielski was able to cite examples of, in his words, 'the perfect harmony of the monorail, integrated with the urban environment' in Seattle. In reality, monorail systems were a concept of the time and a feature of stories in children's comics such as Dan Dare in *The Eagle*. In later years, systems such as the Docklands Light Railway in London and the tramway system in Nottingham, would prove that such concepts could work, but not in Leicester in the 1960s.

In reviewing Smigielski's very detailed and well-argued plans, it is apparent that although he was a gifted architect and planner, he had less understanding of social trends. His was a world seemingly without litter or vandalism, and with unlimited supplies of cheap energy. His world was always sunny. His open landscapes with piazzas have become a reality in a limited way in the Highcross Centre, but there the areas are protected from the elements. For such open spaces to be populated all the year round requires a Mediterranean climate. Yet his shrewd comments on the challenges facing Leicester in the 1960s, a town founded by the Romans, still sound pertinent, and are tinged with eloquent humour:

> Almost since history began cities were congested by traffic. In ancient Rome, streets were so crowded that Caesar forbade any cart traffic from sunrise until dusk and the regulation was strictly enforced. Later, this order (which may remind one of some of the measures being contemplated by Mr Marples, the Minister of Transport) was extended by Marcus Aurelius to every city in the Roman Empire. Goods were brought into the city at night, and the noise of the carts was so great that it condemned the Romans to everlasting insomnia.

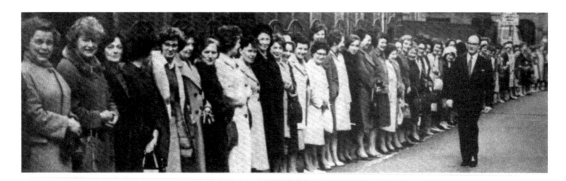

In May 1963, 100 'attractive' women (according to the *Leicester Mercury*) were employed to survey the routine movement of local people. The women were to 'charm their way into hundreds of city homes to ferret out vital information'. Here, Konrad Smigielski appears to be inspecting his female army!

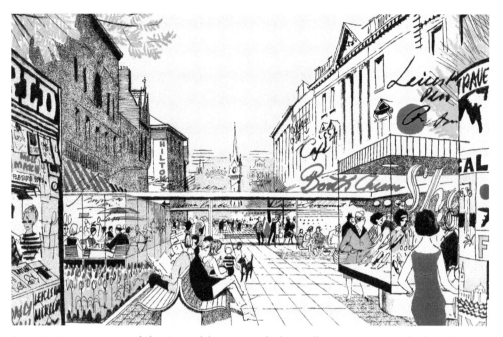

An artist's impression of the Smigielski proposals for Gallowtree Gate, with shop displays extending into the street, but no litter bins in sight.

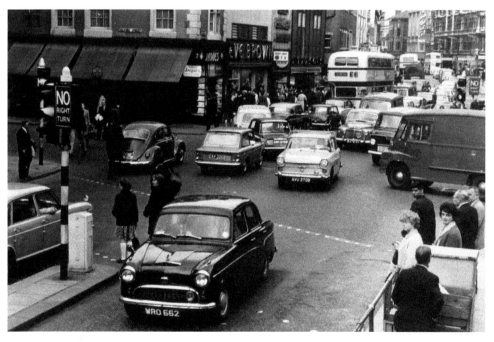

This photograph of the busy Gallowtree Gate, Granby Street, Halford Street and Horsefair Street junction clearly illustrates the congestion problems that Leicester's transport department had to endure. Despite the junction being traffic-light controlled, there is clear conflict of vehicles trying to turn right out of Horsefair Street into Granby Street. The introduction of yellow hatched box junctions was still some time away.

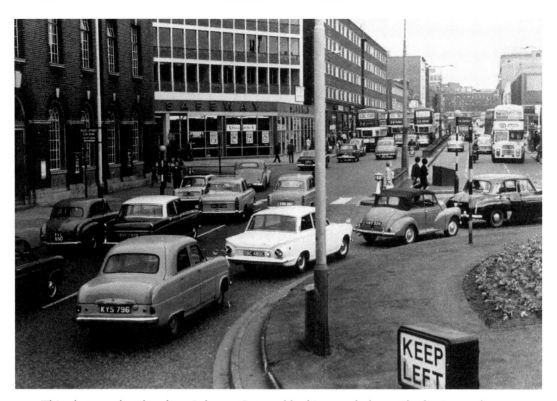

This photograph, taken from Belgrave Gate and looking south down Charles Street, shows a huge variety of car types. Cars circling the roundabout are led by a mid-1950s Humber Hawk, followed by a 1959 Morris Minor convertible, a 1965 Ford Cortina and a 1950s Ford Zephyr 6. The Labour Exchange (now Job Centre) is on the left and the Safeway store under Epic House is also on the left after the entrance to Lower Hill Street. The colours for corporation buses had changed from the mainly maroon to the cream livery in 1961. However, in 1965 there were still many of the older buses still in their original livery.

As part of the research behind the plan, on Tuesday 7 May 1963 100 'attractive' women (according to the *Leicester Mercury*) were sent out onto the streets of Leicester as part of a survey to find out the routine patterns of movement of its inhabitants. The women were to 'charm their way into hundreds of city homes to ferret out vital information'. Other ladies were hired to hand out questionnaires on buses that could be posted back to the council.

Smigielski knew that many of his proposals would be unpalatable. He realised that the public was unlikely to understand the concepts of traffic management he was suggesting. In the summary of proposals in his 1964 plan, he concluded by conceding that he needed popular support if any change was to take place:

> This long-term plan is a practical one and within the financial possibilities of this society; but its realisation will not be easy because the social, economic and administrative implications are profound. The general public will have to change their minds and hearts towards the motor car. They will have to be fully informed about this Plan as without the co-operation of the whole society the realisation of these proposals will not be possible.

Transport

The 1960s was the decade the motor vehicle was to become the principal means of transport in the UK. Petrol rationing had ended in 1950 and over the next ten years the number of car-owning households had increased steadily. It was a new era for motor vehicle design with Sir Alec Issigonis's Mini, launched in 1959, setting a new standard in style, economy and affordability. For the first time, working-class families in Leicester could own the same vehicle as the celebrities of the day, including fashion models such as Twiggy and numerous pop stars. The family version of the Mini, the Austin 1100, appeared in its wake and became Britain's bestselling car for nine consecutive years. In September 1962 another iconic car was launched, the Ford Cortina, followed by a Mark II version four years later. It became Britain's bestselling car in 1967, overtaking sales of the Austin/Morris 1100 and 1300 ranges. In the four evolving versions, Ford's Dagenham plant produced over 933,000 vehicles.

Concurrently, a modernisation plan for the country's ageing rail system had been implemented in 1955 and included the replacement of steam locomotives by diesel and electric power; but by 1960 the railways were losing £68 million a year, rising to £104 million in 1963. Although the number of employees had been reduced by a quarter and more than 3,000 miles of track had been closed, the British railway network was losing more than £300,000 every day.

The response from the government was drastic and immediate. It took the form of the Reshaping of British Railways Report, more commonly known as the 'Beeching Plan', which was published on 27 March 1963. By the end of the decade over 5,600 miles of track had been closed. The former British Railways became British Rail and the emphasis switched to investing in the main trunk routes emanating from London to cities in the Midlands and the North. The price of the new approach was the closure of numerous small branch lines and rural stations such as, in Leicestershire, the station at Kibworth Beauchamp.

If the plan had been accepted in full without amendment, Leicestershire would have lost all its railway stations except Leicester (London Road), Loughborough (Midland), Market Harborough and Melton Mowbray.

In fairness to Dr Beeching, his background research had included consideration of alternative forms of public transport. In this respect his work looked forward to the integrated approach of later decades. He believed that the country's bus services needed more investment and that this form of transport should supply the local transport demands. Leicester City Transport in the 1960s was an efficient and proud operation led by general manager John Cooper until 1966, and then Leslie Smith, in charge until 1975. The managers presided over an extensive fleet of smart double-decker vehicles, but whether Dr Beeching's views on the future role of buses ever reached their ears at Abbey Park Road is a question still to be answered. Both were certainly proud of the fleet and their performance which reflected civic pride in the city. Despite this, both men were keen to move with the times and it was John Cooper who introduced the brighter mainly cream livery in May 1961. This replaced the maroon-and-cream window surrounds livery that had been introduced in 1937.

Leicester City Transport continued to buy, in the main, large capacity double-deckers of the traditional front engine and rear entrance layout throughout most of the 1960s. As an experiment, it purchased three front entrance, rear-engined Leyland Atlantean double-deckers in 1963. It had placed an order with Leyland for a further batch of

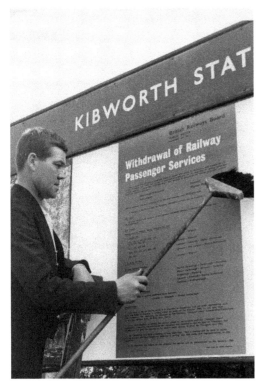

Left: The station in Kibworth Beauchamp on what is now the Midland Mainline was one of several in Leicestershire closed by the Beeching Plan. Goods services ended on 4 July 1966 and the station closed to passengers on 1 January 1968.

Below: The Wigston South Junction signal box, south of Leicester in the days before rail modernisation. It was built in 1900 and closed in 1986.

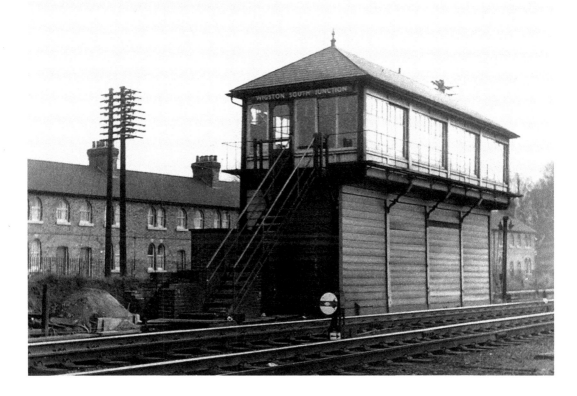

twenty front-engined Leyland PD3s for delivery in 1968/69, but the Labour Government was keen to encourage greater productivity and offered bus grants to vehicles that could be later converted for one man operation. Accordingly, the City Transport department changed its order to twenty Atlanteans that entered service between December 1968 and April 1969. At the end of the decade an increasing number of single-decker buses were purchased – a trend which would continue in the early part of the 1970s.

Another notable City Transport achievement of the 1960s was the introduction of the first Leicester Park and Ride service in 1966. This operated from a car park on Welford Road (opposite Granby Halls) and then followed a loop around Pocklington's Walk, Horsefair Street, Granby Street and Belvoir Street in the city centre. Granby Street was still two-way in 1966. The experimental service operated from 5–24 December 1966 and was considered a great success. In fact, the *Leicester Mercury* described Park 'N' Ride as 'the success of the year'. In February 1967, the Park and Ride service was combined with an existing central area service (the Inner Circle) to operate as a two-way circular service on Mondays to Saturdays. The service was called the 'Centre Circle' and received special identification publicity on stops and vehicles.

The other significant LCT development was the building of a brand new operating centre in Rutland Street to replace the old facilities in Humberstone Gate and Bread Street. These were being demolished in order to build the Haymarket Shopping Centre. The new centre was opened on 9 March 1969.

The other principal bus operator in Leicester during the 1960s was Midland Red. This company had been operating in Leicester since 1922 and concentrated in providing a county-wide network that linked the various villages to the city. Midland Red and the council-owned Leicester City Transport were fierce competitors, but by the 1960s there

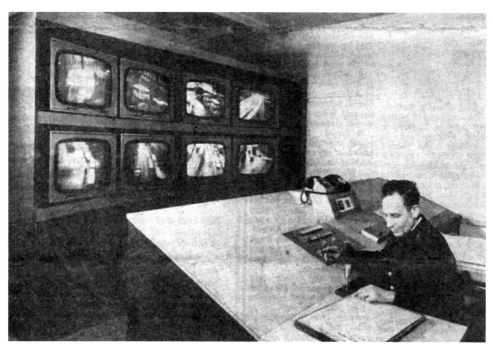

Before the central monitoring of traffic flow by the city's Area Traffic Control system, Leicester City Transport managed their city centre operations from a control room in Rutland Street.

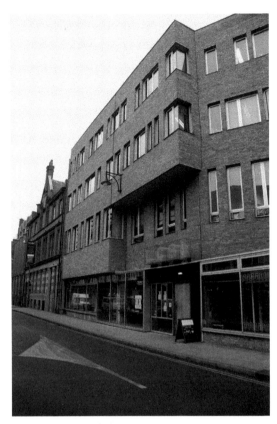

Left: The LCB (Leicester Creative Business) Depot in the city's Cultural Quarter is run by Leicester City Council, and is on the site of the former LCB (Leicester City Bus) Control Centre.

Below: Former Chief Constable Sir Robert Mark introduced traffic wardens to the UK. Based at the city's Charles Street Police Headquarters, they first went on patrol in Leicester in March 1961.

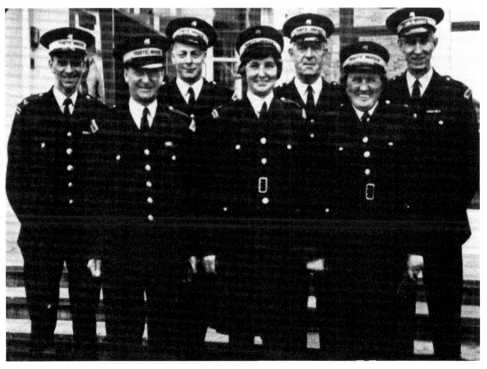

was a mutual realisation that the real competitor to both was the private car and there was a degree of co-operation with jointly operated services in the 1960s.

The reduction of the number of railway stations in Leicestershire and the inevitable increase in road traffic on the major routes into Leicester were factors that came too late for Konrad Smigielski and his traffic plan.

The demise of the Great Central Railway, which connected Leicester with London and with the North, was seen as the largest single closure of the Beeching era, as well as being the most controversial. In a letter published in the *Daily Telegraph* on 28 September 1965, Denis Anthony Brian Butler, 9th Earl of Lanesborough, a peer and railway supporter who lived then at Swithland Hall in Leicestershire, wrote:

> [Among] the main lines in the process of closure, surely the prize for idiotic policy must go to the destruction of the until recently most profitable railway per ton of freight and per passenger carried in the whole British Railways system, as shown by their own operating statistics. These figures were presented to monthly management meetings until the 1950s, when they were suppressed as 'unnecessary', but one suspects really 'inconvenient' for those proposing Beeching type policies of unnecessarily severe contraction of services [...] This railway is of course the Great Central forming a direct Continental loading gauge route from Sheffield and the North to the Thames valley and London for Dover and France.

In January 1960, express passenger services on the Great Central from London to Sheffield through Leicester were discontinued, leaving only three 'semi-fast' London–Nottingham trains each day. In March 1963, local trains on many parts of the route were axed and many rural local stations were closed. Belgrave and Birstall station, near to the Loughborough Road in the city, closed on 1 March 1963. The last passenger train on the Great Central left Leicester on 3 May 1969.

Although more Leicester people were able to afford a motor car in the 1960s, the rail system remained an essential part of life for the thousands of workers in the city's textile, hosiery and dying factors who looked forward to Leicester's annual Industrial Fortnight. In these two weeks at the beginning of July each year, Leicester's industries effectively shut down and the work force en masse headed for the coast by train. It was a time for employees and their managers to relax together, and for families to enjoy the camaraderie of the workplace. Its value in terms of factory floor relationships was invaluable. At the time, this sense of camaraderie could only be achieved through the use of the railway system.

The former Great Northern Railway's Leicester terminus on Belgrave Road, for many decades the 'gateway to Skegness' for Leicester holidaymakers, especially during the Industrial Fortnight in July, closed to these summer specials in September 1962.

It was also the end of the line for the city's first railway station, originally called simply 'Leicester' but later renamed West Bridge. Although rebuilt, this station is thought to have been the third oldest in the world, having opened in 1832. Passenger services had ended in 1928 but freight services still operated on the line until 1979. The station survives only as a single length of platform together with one piece of track and one semaphore signal.

For six years in the 1960s, rail travellers in Leicester were able to experience a taste of luxury rail travel if they were willing to pay the premium fares. The Midland Pullman operated a weekday return service to Leicester from St Pancras between 1960 and 1966. These trains were six-coach diesel-electric multiple-units, a configuration

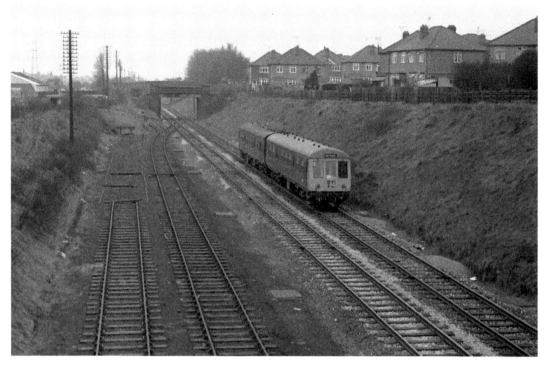

A Rugby to Leicester train in the southern suburbs of Leicester taken from Marlow Road, looking south, on 9 April 1969. After arriving at Leicester Central this train was then due to depart for Nottingham at 7.30 p.m.

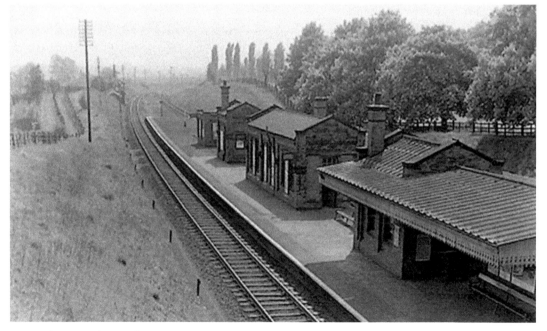

Belgrave and Birstall station on the Great Central Railway photographed in 1962. This is now the heritage line's Leicester North terminus.

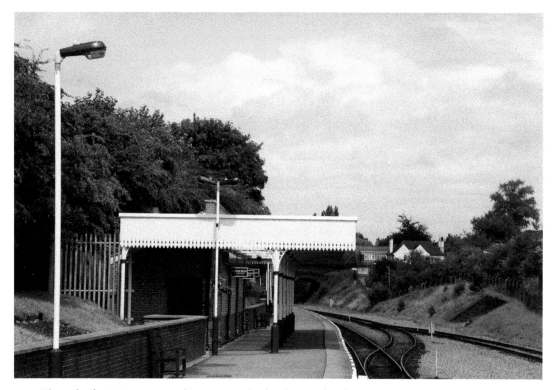

The rebuilt Leicester North station. The bridge in the distance is from where the older photograph was taken.

that was developed later in the highly-successful Inter-city 125 trains. As befitted its name, the Midland Pullman offered luxury, not only in the design of the rolling-stock, with air conditioning and double-glazing, but also in the high level of customer service, having two kitchens serving hot meals to every seat.

The train began its journey each morning in Manchester, reaching London St Pancras in just 3 hours 15 minutes and travelling at 90 mph. It then travelled north to Leicester and Nottingham and returned to St Pancras for the evening return trip back to Manchester. It is significant that Leicester was one of the very few cities connected to the capital by luxury high-speed rail transport in the 1960s, although it is possible that time and scheduling restraints prevented it from serving any city further north on the Midland Main Line such as Sheffield.

The service was introduced to provide a fast north–south service while the East Coast mainline was being electrified. When that project was completed, the new electric services on that line made the Midland Pullman unprofitable.

Shopping

As with so many aspects of life at this time, the shopping experience was beginning to change. The department stores were still offering traditional values and standards of customer service and the main streets in Leicester's central shopping area had seen little change in the brand names above the doors. Marshall and Snelgrove's imposing building, constructed for its previous occupants, the Leicester family business of Adderlys, formerly traders on Leicester Market, dominated Gallowtree Gate with Woolworths, Boots the Chemists and Marks & Spencer on the opposite side of the street.

Lewis's department store occupied much of Humberstone Gate from Fox Lane towards Charles Street with its modernistic tower, which actually dated from when the store was opened in 1936 and still looking very much in keeping with 1960s architectural ideas. On Hotel Street, from its junction with Friar Lane, stood the other great local department store Morgan Squire. In Horsefair Street could be found Simpkin & James; in High Street, or to be precise, Union Street, the rambling Co-op; and with its address as Market Street, the imposing Joseph Johnson & Co. Ltd store that was taken over by Fenwicks in 1962. A true department store, this building was designed by the Leicester Arts and Crafts architect Isaac Barradale, and included living quarters for the female staff on the top floor and a morgue as part of the firm's funeral services in the basement.

The new fashions seemed out of place in the traditional environment, and additionally grocery chains were beginning to make an impression on the High Street in the form of supermarkets. It is claimed that the first supermarket in the UK was the self-service store opened by the Co-op in Manor Park in London on 12 January 1948. Housewives queued in the cold weather outside the store on the opening day. Marks & Spencer introduced

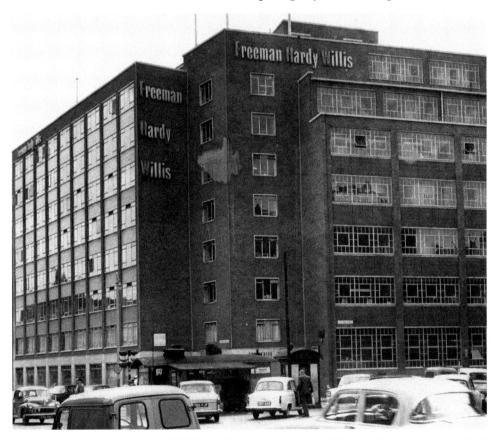

The impressive Freeman Hardy Willis Building on the corner of Rutland Street, photographed in 1963. At one stage, the company, as part of British Shoe Corporation, was the largest shoe retailer in Europe.

a self-service element to their London Wood Green store in 1948 and, two years later, Sainsbury's, also in London, opened their first supermarket. The first Tesco store had opened in London in 1929 and their first supermarket, also in the London area, in 1956.

Leicester's shoppers had to wait until the 1960s before they could sample the new supermarket experience. The Tesco store at Lee Circle in Leicester was to be the company's first retail operation outside London, and when it opened it held the distinction of being the largest store in Europe. Another innovation of the Leicester store was the integrated multi-storey car park. Porters would bring shoppers' purchases directly to the customers' cars. This was regarded so news-worthy that British Pathé filmed a newsreel featuring the car park and store, and reported the innovation nationwide.

Just outside the city, American-owned F. W. Woolworth opened its first Woolco store at Oadby in 1967. The Woolco concept had already been successfully applied in the United States with much larger out-of-town stores. These offered a one-stop shop with plenty of car parking. The Oadby venture was successful and a number of Woolco stores were opened in the UK.

7

SOCIETY, CULTURE AND FAITH

There was no decade in recent centuries where traditional values and assumptions have been challenged so directly than the ten dramatic years of the 1960s.

The 1950s had offered a much sought-after stability following the turmoil of the Second World War. Although many families had continued to experience austerity, there was also a sense of security throughout those years, as families were reunited with their menfolk returning from military service, and the value of family life came to the fore.

Much of the instability that was to occur in the 1960s was centred on the new social trends that encompassed music, fashion, ethics and politics. Young people have challenged their parents' values for centuries, if at times tacitly, but the new mode of challenge expressed itself in intelligent debate, new literature, and new film and theatre. The new ideology had powerful and eloquent voices such as Leicester-born author and philosopher Colin Wilson, whose first novel, *The Outsider,* was published in 1956 when the author was just twenty-four years of age. Wilson's immensely influential *Ritual in the Dark* was published in 1960 and there followed a profusion of short stories and novels.

Wilson identified himself with the 'angry young men' of his time, young writers who were characterised by disillusionment with traditional British society.

Challenging the status quo was not only the province of the academics or the philosophers of the 1960s; it was arguably the first time that popular stars and celebrities such as John Lennon expressed political opinions, and these received at least as much notice as the established writers:

> When I was five years old, my mother always told me that happiness was the key to life. When I went to school, they asked me what I wanted to be when I grew up. I wrote down 'happy'. They told me I didn't understand the assignment, and I told them they didn't understand life.

Politics

In the closing months of the previous decade, Harold Macmillan led the Conservative Party to its third consecutive election victory and a majority of 100 over the Labour Party. This was despite imposing a unilateral wage freeze in 1961 as an attempt to deal with an increasing balance of payments deficit. He went on to make major Cabinet changes in 1962, an event now referred to as the 'night of the long knives' when eight junior ministers were sacked. The Profumo Scandal in 1963 permanently damaged the credibility of Macmillan's government, and in October of that year he resigned the leadership of the party. The Foreign Secretary, Alec Douglas-Home, went to the country just twelve months later.

On 15 October 1964, Labour came to power with a majority of just four seats and a new leader, Harold Wilson, who had led the party through the election campaign following the sudden death of Hugh Gaitskell at the age of fifty-six. The majority proved to be unworkable and Wilson went to the country again in 1966, this time securing a comparatively substantial majority of ninety-six seats. Both Conservative and Labour governments in the 1960s struggled with the country's economic decline, the steady increase in imported consumer goods, and a consequent widening trade gap.

The Wilson Administration between 1964 and 1970 was a reforming government that addressed a number of major social issues. These included the abolition of the death penalty in 1965 and the liberalisation of laws on abortion, censorship, divorce, homosexuality and immigration. The capital punishment issue was to last for five years, but in the closing days of the decade abolition was made permanent. All three party leaders, Prime Minister Harold Wilson, the Conservative leader Edward Heath and Liberal leader Jeremy Thorpe supported permanent abolition.

In 1969, the Suffrage of the People Act gave young people aged between eighteen and twenty-one the right to vote, but not to stand as parliamentary candidates. In the general election that followed, in June 1970, the Conservatives returned to power under Edward Heath.

Leicester was represented in Parliament by four men, three whose loyalties were with the moderate elements of the Labour Party and one Conservative who had links with Britain's colonial past. The MP for Leicester North East for twenty-one years from 1962 until 1983 (which involved the new constituency of Leicester East from 1974) was Tom Bradley, who represented the moderate right of the Labour Party and also served as the President of the moderate white-collar Transport Salaried Staffs' Association. In Leicester North West stood Barnett Janner, a former Lord Mayor of Leicester who was succeeded by his son, Greville Janner, in 1970.

Herbert William Bowden, another former local councillor, was the MP for Leicester South West until 1967. When Labour came to power in 1964, Bowden was appointed Leader of the House of Commons and Lord President of the Council. In 1966 he was moved to the new post of Secretary of State for Commonwealth Affairs and in 1967 was made a life peer as Baron Aylestone of Aylestone. He later became chairman of the Independent Television authority, and was succeeded in his Leicester seat by Tom Boardman (Conservative).

Sir William 'John' Peel was the Conservative Member for Leicester South East, following a career in the colonial service and surviving imprisonment by the Japanese during the Second World War when he had been stationed in Singapore. His father had been Governor of Hong Kong and he served as British Resident in Brunei and Resident Commissioner of the Gilbert and Ellice Islands. His one moment of controversy came in 1959 in the House of Commons, when during a debate on the Mau Mau rebellion in Kenya, he stated that 'there are obvious risks in dealing with desperate and sub-human individuals'. In the discussion that continued, it was emphasised that Britain would show the same attitude and respect for all people regardless of their nationality. It was an inappropriate remark to be spoken by someone who was representing an increasingly diverse constituency, but Peel was also an early and strong advocate for the UK's involvement in Europe.

Health, Fitness and Food

The family diet changed considerably in the years between the post-war period of austerity and rationing, and the widening of choice and pre-packaged foods of the supermarkets in the 1970s. In the 1960s, most of a family's food purchases were made at corner shops or local greengrocers, where choice was limited. There were very few ready-cooked meals, and for many, the staple diet was the very English 'meat and two veg'.

There was little emphasis on healthy eating or an awareness of excess fat, salt and sugar intake. Family dinners would include meat pies covered in pastry, bread and butter puddings, suet pudding and meat with the fat kept on. All milk was whole milk. Few working-class families ever ate out in restaurants or cafés except during their annual holiday, and pubs in Leicester tended to serve very little food except for the inevitable potato crisps. Golden Wonder, based in Market Harborough, launched its first flavoured crisps – cheese and onion – in 1962.

In Leicester, as in other cities and towns in the UK, but more notably in London and the south-east, many new Indian restaurants opened during the 1960s. This was caused, not only by the rise in immigration from the Indian subcontinent, but also because it was now easier to obtain the spices needed for Asian cooking. The first Indian and Chinese takeaways became available.

So-called 'instant' foods were beginning to be seen on the shelves of grocery shops. In 1967, Angel Delight was launched, originally marketed as a health food. It was a powdered mixture of whey powder, sugar and starches, to which some gelling agents and flavourings had been added. It was targeted at the working-class parents of the 1960s who, it was claimed by marketing researchers, had little time to spend cooking in the kitchen.

Vesta curries and Vesta chow mein were the first taste of foreign food for many people. The Vesta range is still remembered with fondness by those who were children in the 1960s, despite the food's appearance. One memory recorded by an oral history website is representative of many similar comments:

> It looked like a tray full of string and cardboard with some chopped up rubber, but tasted divine. I can still taste the monosodium glutamate to this day!

Home Life

Many thousands of Victorian terraced houses were replaced during the 1960s using new design concepts and new materials. Wooden window frames would continue, but in many new homes these were being replaced by more durable metal units. In kitchens, the old work surfaces were being superseded by plastics such as Formica, a form of melamine which could be cleaned easily and were therefore more hygienic. White goods were becoming more available and affordable, including fridges and washing machines. For many families, there was an appetite for modernity.

The increasing wealth of many working-class families enabled more people to buy their own homes, often making use of local government mortgages with reasonable rates of interest. Those who acquired older properties sought to modernise them, or at least to make them look modern within the limitations of each family's finances. Fireplaces were gradually removed or boxed in, the coal fire being replaced by electric or gas heaters. Fitted carpets were beginning to cover the linoleum floors and the dark, heavy furniture and fittings of the previous decades were being replaced by lighter and brighter designs. Fashions were to follow this same trend from the dark traditional sameness of the past to the very brightest of colours and most bizarre of designs. Similarly, the family car was no longer black but could be purchased in any number of bright colours.

The bright new world was not within the reach of everyone. Despite the slum clearances, many who were children in the 1960s remembered having baths in front of the coal fire in the living room, or walks in freezing weather to the toilet at the bottom of the yard or garden, and a general atmosphere of 'make do and mend'. For the children of fathers who were in regular employment it was a time of much improved prosperity, of having more toys than their parents had, as well as more clothes and an increasing variety of sweets, treats and food.

New Cultures

Leicester has been a diverse city for many decades and its journey towards being the first city with a minority white population has been a complex one, but it was to be in the 1960s that the future racial composition of Leicester would be defined. As early as 1936, people from the Basque region of Spain moved to the area, settling in Evington. During the late 1940s and early 1950s, ex-servicemen from the Caribbean as well as new migrants from the various Caribbean islands began to settle in the Highfields area of Leicester, and in the 1950s the first Chinese families moved to Leicester, many moving into the catering industry. Polish people began moving into Leicester in 1939 at the beginning of the Second World War and have continued to settle in the city ever since. After the war, many Polish men serving with the British army found they could not return to Poland, as by then it had been occupied by the Soviet Union. As a result, many Poles (130,000) settled in the UK. Living mostly in the Highfields area of Leicester, the community set up a Polish church and a Polish club that are still both active today.

The independence of India from the British Empire in 1947 resulted in the division of the subcontinent and the uprooting of over 10 million people. More than 1 million people died in the violence and many sought a peaceful life elsewhere including the UK. Arguably the most significant factor was the 1948 British Nationality Act, which technically gave every Commonwealth citizen the right to move to Britain. Given the demand for workers in Britain in the post-war years, there was a strong incentive to migrate. Indians and Pakistanis moved chiefly into properties in the Belgrave and Spinney Hill areas of Leicester where affordable private housing was available.

Between 1965 and 1967, about 23,000 people of Indian origin were forced to leave Kenya following restrictions placed on them by Jomo Kenyatta, the leader of the newly independent Kenyan Government. Concerns about the numbers of Kenyan Asians fleeing to Britain were legislated for in the Commonwealth Immigration Act of 1968, preventing those not directly descended from a British-born person from moving to the UK.

When, in 1972, General Idi Amin of Uganda began to expel the country's Asian population, many believed that Leicester would be a suitable place in which to rebuild their lives because of the existing Asian population. The Belgrave and Melton Road 'Golden Mile' and Rushey Mead became the specific areas of the city where these new migrants would settle.

BBC Radio Leicester in 1967 was clearly already aware of the substantial potential Asian and Indian audiences. The station in its launch publicity promised 'programmes for immigrants', using the terminology of the time, and from the start it broadcast a

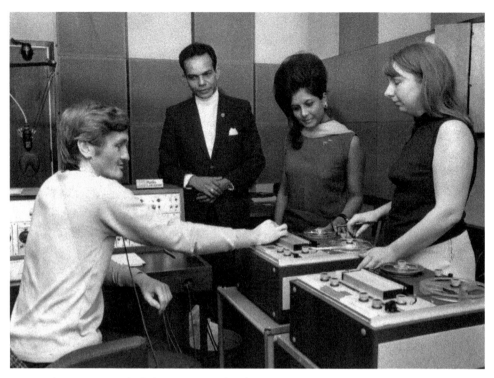

BBC Radio Leicester included programmes for the Leicester Asian community in its launch-week output. In this photograph from 1968, Mr Nazim Muradali and his wife, Mrs Vidya Pooran-Muradali, from Trinidad, are with station assistant Dave Kirkwood and Rita Chapman, the producer of the 'Programme for Immigrants'. Nazim Muradali was an MP in Trinidad and at one time a popular radio announcer. He still serves as a JP. His late wife was formerly the Principal of ASJA Girls College in San Fernando.

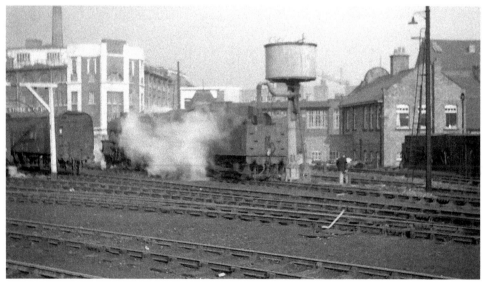

The Great Central station in 1965. The view is from the south of the station looking towards Great Central Street.

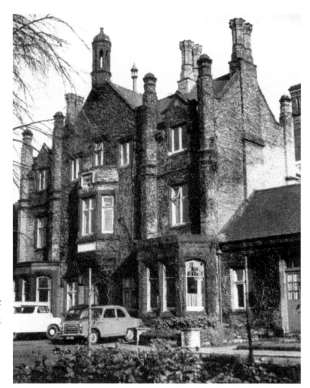

Hillcrest Hospital was formerly the Leicester Union workhouse. This was Leicester's main geriatric unit until its closure in 1977. Many visitors were shocked at the state of the building and the all too obvious remnants of its past role. In 1972, a refugee Asian Ugandan family was accommodated in the former cell block.

weekly programme called *Milan*, which in Hindi can be translated as 'a coming together', presented by a local Sikh, Kartar Singh Sandhu.

Protest and the World Vision

International neuroses and anxieties began when Europe was recovering from the Second World War and citizens came to accept or refuse the many new national boundaries. On 13 August 1961 construction began on the Berlin Wall. In the same year, the Cuban Missile Crisis forced many millions of people to contemplate nuclear war. The Soviet Union was discovered to be installing nuclear missiles in Cuba, just 90 miles from the American coast. A telephone hotline was set up between Washington and Moscow for the first time to allow the leaders to talk to each other directly.

Although the Soviet Union pulled back from action at a very late stage, the governments in both the East and the West knew that a nuclear war had been only very narrowly averted. The Soviet missiles were taken out of Cuba and shortly afterwards US missiles already based in Turkey were also removed. In 1962 a ban on nuclear testing in the atmosphere was agreed between the United States, the Soviet Union and Britain. International tension relaxed as the immediate threat of nuclear war faded away.

Responding to the build-up of nuclear weapons, the Campaign for Nuclear Disarmament had been launched in London in February 1958, and the first Easter Aldermaston March in that year attracted much media attention.

From the mid-1960s nuclear issues were increasingly replaced as the subject of mass popular protest by anger over the United States' war on Vietnam. CND continued as a

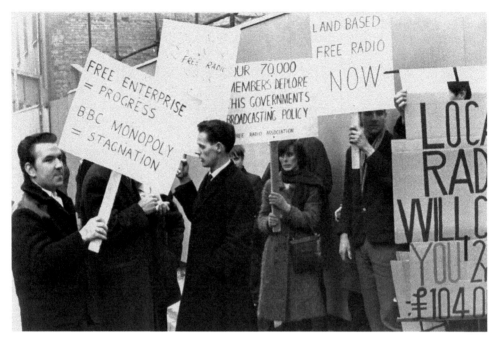

Campaigners opposed to the government's Marine and Broadcasting (Offences) Act staged a protest in Lower Hill Street on 8 November 1967, the day that BBC Radio Leicester began broadcasting.

much smaller movement but protests continued, particularly in Scotland, where British nuclear-armed submarines were now based. The Leicester branch of CND, working with other local organisations with similar aims, such as Amnesty International, has been a regular presence at Leicester's clock tower and at public events such as the City of Leicester Show.

In 1963, the western world was rocked by the assassination of President John F. Kennedy. The Cultural Revolution in China, set in motion by Mao Zedon, began in May 1967 – the cultural year of 'flower power' and peace in the West – and in the closing years of the decade the troubles that were to continue for more than a quarter of a century began in Northern Ireland.

Religion

Leicester and Leicestershire's remarkable willingness to draw in to its community those with radically differing political and religious ideologies is well known, as is the association with the city of so many reformers. In the fourteenth century John Wycliffe came to Lutterworth under the protection of John of Gaunt after preaching his Lollard theology, and was rector of the town from 1374 until his death in 1384. The protestant reformer Hugh Latimer was born in Thurcaston. George Fox, the founder of the Society of Friends or Quakers, was born in Fenny Drayton in Leicestershire, the son of Puritan parents. In the eighteenth century John Jennings established an academy for dissenters in Kibworth Harcourt. William Carey, the pioneer Baptist missionary and founder of the Baptist Missionary Society, moved from Northamptonshire to Leicester in 1783 to become minister of the Harvey Lane chapel, and Robert Hall was another significant leader of the Baptist denomination who followed in Carey's footsteps. He was active during a period of great expansion in the Baptist movement. Hall was born at Arnesby in the south of the county and went to school in Wigston.

However, despite this diversity, faith in Leicester at the beginning of the 1960s was overwhelming Christian and white, with worship in either a parish church, a Nonconformist chapel or as a Roman Catholic. The majority of Leicester's inhabitants were content to be described, if nominally, as 'Christian'. The then Bishop of Leicester, the Right Revd Ronald Williams, acknowledged that the city's industrial past had created a strong Nonconformist tradition, so much so that in the nineteenth century, it was described as 'radical Leicester'. Writing in a national newspaper, in 1969, he also demonstrated his awareness of the changes that were happening as a result of inward migration:

> All are aware of large non-Christian communities living in their midst – Pakistanis, Hindus, Muslims and Sikhs. This year many Christians joined these religions in honour of Mahatma Ghandi.

Williams also acknowledged that the beginning of a truly multi-cultural city was happening 'on his watch', and while celebrating all the positive activities taking place in church congregations across the diocese, he added a note of concern:

> A special problem has of course presented itself with the arrival of many thousands of coloured migrants. The Revd E. W. Carlisle has made St Peter's Church [in Highfields] a warm-hearted centre for those willing to be identified as Christians, and has been at the heart of wider community efforts for the whole immigrant community.

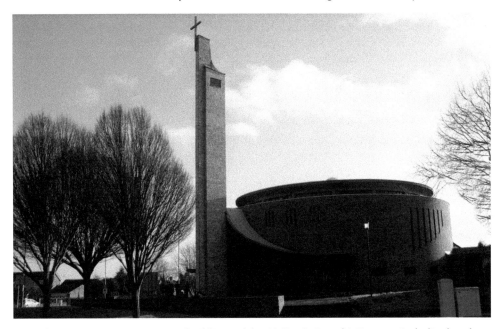

One of Leicester's most innovative buildings of the 1960s, St Joseph's Roman Catholic church on the corner of Uppingham Road and Goodwood Road was constructed in 1968. It was designed by architect Tom Wilson in an open circular plan and with a central altar. Wilson's son, Thomas, has an architectural practice in Oakham, Rutland.

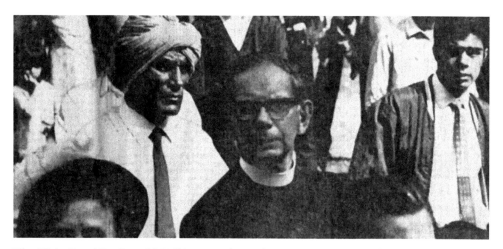

The Right Revd Dr Ronald Williams, Bishop of Leicester, attending the Mahatma Gandhi Centennial in Leicester in 1969.

Those who were 'not willing to be identified as Christians' began to open their own places of worship representing the faiths of the incoming communities. The first Islamic Centre in Leicester was established in 1968 – in a house in St Peter's Road and near to the parish church – by a group of Pakistani Sunni Muslims. The Centre is still based at No. 2A Sutherland Street. The first Hindu temple in Leicester was in Cromford Street, also in Highfields. It was opened in 1969. The first Sikh Gurdwara also opened during this decade, the Guru Nanak Dev Ji Gurdwara later moving to its present location in Holy Bones.

In the twenty-first century, Leicester's places of worship include buildings that serve almost the entire world's faiths, including Baha'i, Buddhism, Christianity, Hinduism, Islam, Jainism, Judaism, and Sikhism.

Class

Researchers and sociologists still debate the effects on Britain's class structure that were caused by the profound social changes that took place in the 1960s. The Labour Government was certainly convinced that the education system was failing children from working-class families, and began looking at the comprehensive system as a more equitable way forward, although class barriers appeared to stay fixed in further education and the number of working-class children going to university later in the decade actually decreased.

The former relatively clear-cut perceptions of landed gentry, a rich business and upper-management class, an aspiring skilled middle class and a largely unskilled working class were beginning to fade. In Leicester, increased prosperity as a result of near-full employment enabled many working-class families to acquire the indicators of the middle classes, including a car, new furniture and fittings in the home, and a house of their own in the leafy suburbs.

Researchers at the time looked for dividing lines between social groups, but outside the workplace found little evidence of an awareness, for instance, of a distinction between the shop floor and the office. However, despite the growing prosperity, poverty still existed, and there remained clear class distinctions in health of Leicester

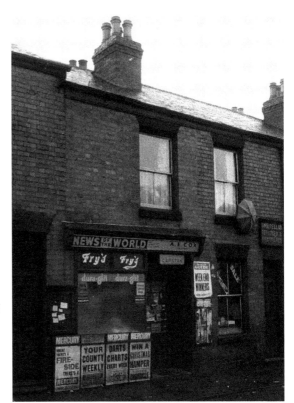

By 1960, many buildings in the area of Clipstone Street near Upper Conduit Street had been demolished or were empty and awaiting redevelopment. Annie E. Cox was still the newsagent at No. 55. Next door was umbrella maker Albert Walker.

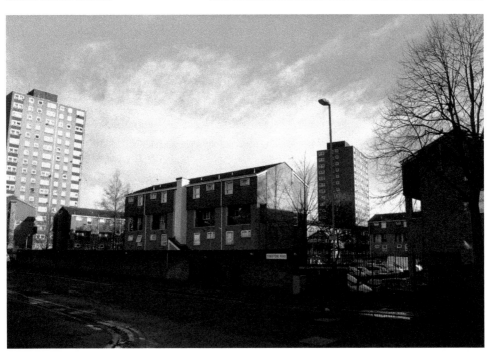

The view from Hutchinson Street in 2015 towards the previous junction with Clipstone Street. The street ran from where the railings now stand to the right of the street sign for Maidstone Road.

residents. At the lower end of the social spectrum, life was still on the breadline and failed to improve despite the obvious signs of a thriving economy.

The discontent that this fostered would be seen in other cities through a rise in strong Socialist ideologies, and the crippling strikes called by the trade unions which were gaining support, more members and therefore more power. Throughout the decade, many workers were engaged in struggles that impacted on the lives of millions through their trade unions.

The Generation Gap

The new pop culture also challenged previous class distinctions. Young fashion designers and musicians followed in the footsteps of The Beatles and the other new beat groups in moving from a working-class background to unimaginable riches, and changed their lifestyles too. Many of the young people who followed these icons, aspired to the similar wealth and fame, and began to disassociate themselves from the moral code of the previous decades with its perceived inequality and prejudices. The 'generation gap' was beginning to widen. The older generation not only could not understand the new music and new values, but also mistrusted them. Many parents were concerned at the near reverence with which their children followed the pronouncements of the pop stars and their willing acceptance of their ethics and more liberal moral values. In many Leicester households, the teenagers were told that pop music was a 'passing fad' and that the long-haired, guitar-playing young men, together with the miniskirted 'dolly-birds', would one day 'get a proper job'.

Fashion

Before the 1960s, fashion in the western world had been dictated by well-known designers working in London and Paris. The fundamental change was that in the future fashion design would be influenced by the 'ordinary' men and women in society. It would set the general mood for the remainder of the twentieth century.

When designer Mary Quant launched her miniskirt in 1964, fashion for young people was changed forever and Britain became the leader in design. The miniskirt was eventually to be worn by nearly every stylish young woman in the western world and represented a major shift in the way people would dress. Hemlines kept rising and by 1968 had reached well above mid-thigh. These were known as 'micro-minis'. This was when the 'angel dress' made its appearance on the fashion scene, a micro-mini dress with a flared skirt and long sleeves, usually worn with patterned tights.

The 1960s were years of fashion innovation and were notable for the introduction of trousers for women. Traditionally, trousers had been viewed by western societies as masculine, but by the beginning of the decade it became acceptable for women to wear them. Women appreciated the garment's practicality, comfort and versatility. In terms of fashion, they could be worn with tunics, shawls and jackets, and they came in many styles – narrow, wide, below the knee, above the ankle, and eventually mid-thigh. These mid-thigh cut trousers were a later evolution that became the modern shorts. Certainly, trousers were also worn as a statement by women who wished to voice their equality to men; in the later years of the 1960s another style was created that was accepted by those who promoted sexual liberation and a political stance of 'peace, love and freedom'.

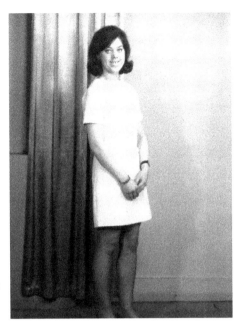

Possibly the most easily defined fashion styles since the Second World War were those of the 1960s. This photograph, taken in studios in Granby Street, Leicester, shows young Gwynneth Brooks in the typical fashion of her teenage years. The date is August 1968.

At the same time a more androgynous style of clothing was in vogue. Both men and women were able to wear frayed bell-bottomed jeans, tie-dyed shirts, work shirts and headbands. Wearing sandals was also part of a 'hippie' look for both men and women. Concurrent with these broader influences, hairstyles also changed, and men and women began to wear their hair in similar styles. It became fashionable for women to wear their hair short.

Multiculturalism in fashion was also popular with much inspiration in terms of style and design being from the traditional clothing of countries including Nepal, India, Bali, Morocco and parts of the African continent. Ponchos, moccasins, love beads, peace signs and medallion necklaces were all accessories that connected with these influences.

Women's Liberation

After the Second World War, as the men returned from military service to civilian life, it was assumed and expected that women would also make the return to their previous 'natural role' within the family. As a result, women were excluded from the debate over rates of pay, hours of work and the nature of employment. The Beveridge Report in 1942 based many of its assertions on the traditional gender roles and that women's primary role was that of homemaker and childrearing.

The laudable principle of the new welfare state was to provide the same benefits to all, regardless of class or gender, effectively redistributing wealth, privileges and benefits equally, but the system was still based on women being at home and men going out to work. Even the school day assumed that women worked primarily in the home and were dependent economically on the husband's wages. Such assumptions were emphasised in the classroom in the different subjects that children were taught.

The Women's Liberation Movement began to form in the closing years of the decade. Women's movements campaigning for change had been active in Leicester since the suffragettes of the nineteenth century but ceased with the outbreak of the First World

War. Many of Leicester's left-wing communities were therefore historically very supportive of women's rights. Protests at the Miss America pageants in 1968 and 1969 were followed by similar direct actions at the Miss World competition in London on 20 November 1970. This was a movement that had been gathering strength throughout the previous years and had included a strike in 1968 by female machinists at the Dagenham plant of Ford demanding equal pay, and supported by a new organisation – the National Joint Action Committee on Women's Equal Rights.

The Labour Government believed that a rise in the employment of women would be a way to address the labour shortages of the time, and that such a strategy was more acceptable than the alternative of encouraging further immigration in order to fill job vacancies.

Magazine design and fashion photography in the 1960s presented a new feminine ideal for women and young girls in the form of the 'single girl'. She was portrayed as young, single, active and self-sufficient in terms of her emotional needs. New models such as Jean Shrimpton became icons by portraying this new 'perfect' young woman with the ideal figure, but the aspirations that such imagery fostered were to lead to a lifetime of diets and other psychological constraints.

However, for some years to come the traditional attitudes of male culture were to prevail. In Leicester, women were the mainstay of the textile, hosiery and boot and shoe trades, but not to be seen in the management offices. The public services and the political environment were dominated by men. In the health sector, women staffed the wards of the Leicester Royal Infirmary, the Groby Road Hospital and the General Hospital, but most of the doctors, surgeons and management were male.

The BBC, in the form of Radio Leicester, seemingly endorsed the status quo in terms of the role of women in society and the workplace when it was launched in 1967. The station promised 'programmes for women' and, by definition, apparently none for men, suggesting that women would not wish to listen to the news or follow the sports coverage. The station, apparently believing that women had a different musical taste to that of men, promised:

> Women will get their own feature every weekday morning covering fashion, shopping, home hints, etc. and there will be a special record requests programme for them.

Their 'own feature' was called 'Coffee Break' and ran for 45 minutes from 10.30 a.m. each morning, carefully timed to provide a break in the female listeners' daily household chores. There was also the tacit assumption that women enjoyed a different type of music than their menfolk and they needed help with their shopping and household duties. BBC Radio Leicester also proposed a 'Keep Fit for Women' programme, but this never reached the airwaves. All the principal presenters, producers and management of the station when it opened were male, although Wendy Blair presented a number of programmes including 'Coffee Break', and one of the station assistants (technical operators) was Janet Cufflin.

In the ten years from 1960, only nine women were newly elected to parliament. The only woman elected to parliament from Leicestershire before the 1990s was Miss Irene Mervyn Pike (Conservative), who represented the Melton constituency from 1956 until 1974. She was created a life peer as Baroness Pike in 1974. The only female MP to serve a Leicester constituency in the entire twentieth century was Patricia Hewitt, who was elected to parliament in 1997 succeeding Greville Janner.

8

OVER THE HORIZON

It had been a dramatic decade and Leicester had changed in so many ways over ten remarkable years. In the closing days of the final year of the decade, on 15 December 1969, *The Times* newspaper published a supplement promoting the city of Leicester, which was titled 'Leicester: A Special Report'. The main article was written by the distinguished historian from Leicester University, Professor Jack Simmons. His overview of the city and its relationship with the county of Leicestershire was titled 'Roots in the Family Business'.

The making of shoes, socks and light engineering was given as the city's main industries. Simmons described the lively market and the enthusiastic support of local people for their principal sporting teams – Leicester City and Leicester Tigers – and he wrote of how the character of modern Leicester is derived from its historic past:

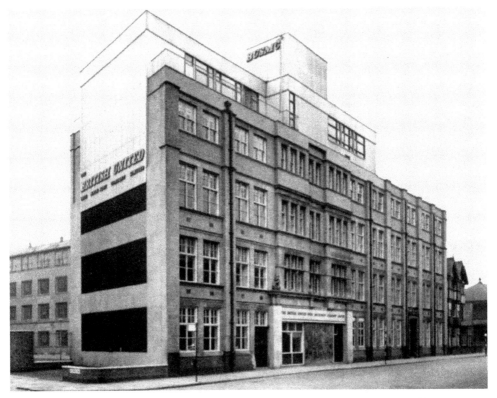

The British United Shoe Machinery Co. in 1965, then employing over 4,500 staff in Leicester. The building is now home to several small businesses as the Belgrave Commercial Centre.

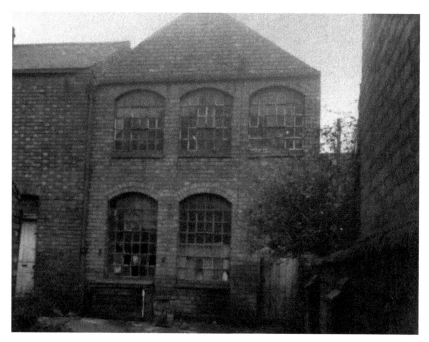

The rear of a small factory building in Haverlock Street near to the Leicester Royal Infirmary. The area has undergone major redevelopment but some of the earlier Victorian buildings have survived into the twenty-first century.

To a degree unusual for a great industrial town it is the product of a long evolution, to be traced back almost continuously for two thousand years. Apart from the sieges it suffered in 1173 and 1645 its history has been little interrupted by violence. Its life has been a story of steady continuous adaptation to changing circumstances and opportunities.

The final article in the supplement was written by the then Bishop of Leicester, the Right Revd Dr Ronald Williams. He spoke of Leicester's religious history, tracing it from the third century to the time he was writing, and underlining the strong tradition of religion-based charity, citing the Elizabethan Wyggeston's Hospital, the Mission for the Deaf and the Samaritans of the present day.

In 1969, the bishop was also mindful of the challenge presented by immigration, and praised the incumbent of St Peter's church for creating a warm-hearted centre for those willing to be identified as Christians [which is] at the heart of wider community efforts for the whole immigrant community:

> Leicester still keeps some of its traditions, one of which is a marked spirit of good will towards the religion it has known for at least 1,500 years, and a strong social conscience, combined with a sturdy refusal to be dragooned into too much churchgoing or involved in too much generosity by those whose duty it is to engage in such irritating activities.

The veteran BBC journalist Roland Orton described the employment prospects for Leicester people. He presented the remarkable statistic that if every job advertised at the local employment exchange was to be taken by a local person, only forty people would remain out of work.

Leicester was still a city of relative prosperity, with textiles at its heart. However, he noted the decline in the membership of the Leicester Footwear Manufacturers Association, warning of future problems in that industry yet concluded his article on a positive note:

> Whatever the future holds for hosiery and shoes, one thing seems assured – the variety of trades in Leicester and district, spearheaded by a thrusting engineering industry, assures a continuance of the conditions which make it one of the busiest and most prosperous cities in Britain.

It was an optimist forecast. The 1970s would be beset by economic problems and the decline of many of Leicester's staple manufacturing industries, leading to the dark days of the 'Winter of Discontent' of 1978–79 when the lights went out in Leicester and other cities in the UK. The city survived, largely because of the large number of smaller industries and businesses that could ride the economic waves and provide employment. In 1969, Professor Jack Simmons looked to the city's past in order to provide some reassurance of its future prosperity in the new decade:

> Its history has been little interrupted by violence. It was fortunate in escaping any major damage from air raids. Its life has been a story of steady continuous adaptation to changing circumstances and opportunities.

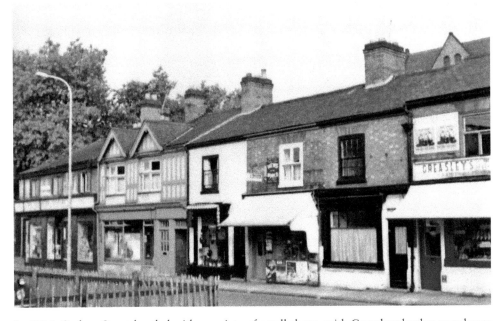

In 1965, Carlton Street bustled with a variety of small shops, with Greasleys leather merchants (at No. 19), Watts Newsagents (No. 23), Hibbert's Furniture Shop (No. 27), Herbert Dunn, Baker (No. 29), and the Corner Stores on the corner of Infirmary Square. In 1965 this was a street with a rich variety of shops and services. The road is now part of the Welford Road–Oxford Street gyratory.

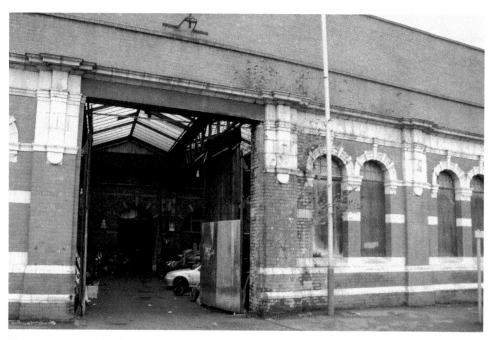

The Great Central Railway's Leicester station, in 2015 housing a multitude of small businesses.

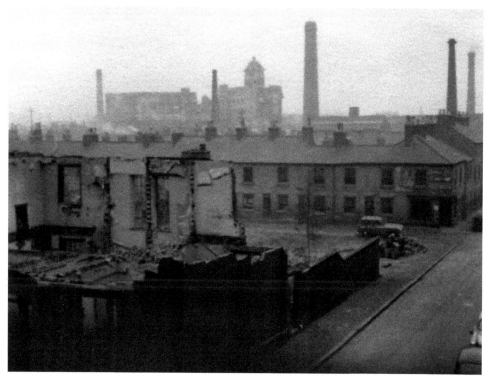

Thomas Hunting's corner shop can be seen on the corner of Goswell Street and Middle Street. The demolition of this area was to make way for the Fletcher Building of Leicester Polytechnic. Most of the homes had been empty since the mid-1950s.

An advertisement in a national newspaper taken out by the Corporation of the City of Leicester towards the end of the decade declared that Leicester was open for business and ready for the future:

> Leicester – a city for Britain to be proud of. Prosperous, yes – but a city that works hard for its prosperity. Ten 'Queen's Awards to Industry' to date. For making good things and selling them actively. Overseas. Where it matters. This is the new patriotism. Trying that bit harder for the good of all Britain. And Leicester is leading the way.

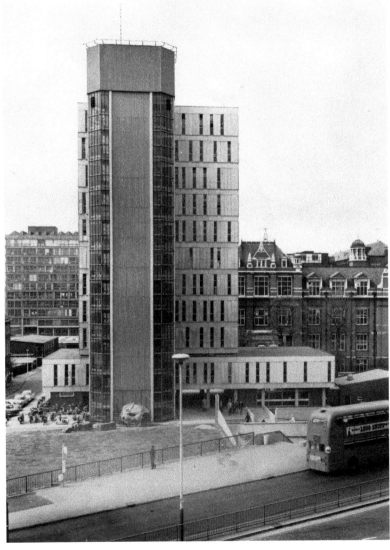

Three distinctive buildings that were a part of the 1960s Leicester skyline. Behind the James Went Building, demolished in 2004, is the Victorian frontage of the first stage of the Hawthorn Building, and the high rise element of the Fletcher Building, all part of Leicester Polytechnic when this photograph was taken in the early 1960s.

SOURCES

Beasley, B., *Post-War Leicester* (The History Press, 2006).

Cockburn, C., *Antimilitarism: Political and Gender Dynamics of Peace Movements* (Palgrave MacMillan, 2012)

Centenary History of the School of Textiles (Leicester Polytechnic Press, 1983).

Dyer, R., *Heavenly Bodies: Film Stars and Society* (London: Routledge, 2013).

Lambert, D. *The History of Leicestershire County Cricket Club* (London: Christopher Helm, 1992).

'Leicester: A Special Report', *The Times*, 15 December 1969.

Newsome, R., *The Modern Brass Band: From the 1930s to the Millenium* (Hants: Ashgate Publishing Ltd, 2006).

Simmons, J., *Leicester and its University* (Leicester University Press, 1963).

Williams, C., *Bishop's Wife But Still Myself* (London: George Allen & Unwin Ltd, 1961).

Williams, D. (ed.), *The Adaptation of Change: Essays Upon the History of Nineteenth-Century Leicester and Leicestershire* (Leicestershire Archaeological and Historical Society and Leicestershire Museums, Art Galleries and Records Service, 1980).

ACKNOWLEDGEMENTS

I must record my grateful thanks to my father, George Butt, who has taken a great interest in this project and who corrected the first draft. I must also acknowledge the involvement of Robert Kemp, Chris Jinks and Mike Greenwood of the Leicester Transport Heritage Trust, who read the text and offered many valuable comments and suggestions especially relating to transport. Also to the many people who have verified specific details and provided specialist information, including Cathy Wilson of the Royal Institute of British Architects Library and Information Centre, John Skinner (Speedway History) and Gerald Clode (Leicester Rediffusion).

    I acknowledge the ownership and sources of the photographs reproduced in this book, which include Robert Smith, Denis Calow, Ben Brooksbank, Sam Holmes, Kibworth History Society, *Leicester Mercury*, University of Leicester, BBC Radio Leicester, John Daniell (Leicester Museums), Dr Neil Clifton, Nigel Tout and Gerald Clode (Rediffusion, Leicester). I would like to especially acknowledge the kind help of Katharine Short, the archivist at De Montfort University, who provided scans of a number of fascinating images from that institution's remarkable collections.

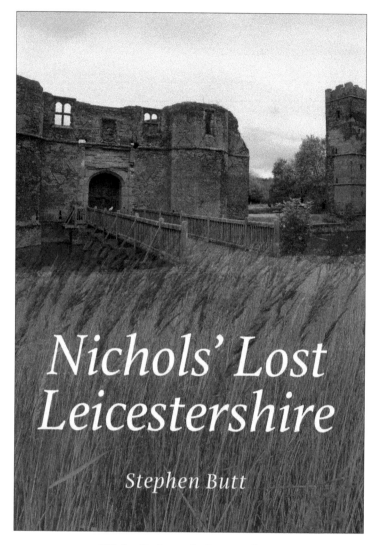

Nichol's Lost Leicestershire

Stephen Butt

John Nichols' monumental *History and Antiquities of the County of Leicester* has been the foundation of historical research in Leicestershire. Stephen Butt celebrates this devotion and commitment to the county by looking at how the 200-year-old architecture has survived to present day.

978 1 4456 2077 0